D0043194

MEE
Speaks

MEE Speaks

But Does She Have Anything to Say?

Mary Ellen Edmunds

DESERET BOOK

Salt Lake City, Utah

Library of Congress Cataloging-in-Publication Data

Edmunds, Mary Ellen, 1940-
  MEE speaks / Mary Ellen Edmunds.
      p. cm.
  ISBN 978-1-59038-887-7 (pbk.)
  1. Christian life—Mormon authors.   I. Title.
BX8656.E357 2008
248.4'89332—dc22   2007046815

Printed in the United States of America
Lifetouch

10   9   8   7   6   5   4   3   2   1

Contents

Preface

Recently someone asked me, "How many talks have you given?" I've never tried to come up with a total, but it might be quite a few. I've had the blessing of teaching and speaking at the Missionary Training Center for many years, along with Know Your Religion, Especially for Youth, Education Week, BYU Women's Conference, and so on.

The idea for this book came because I kept having requests for copies of talks I've given. So I've created this collection of talks and parts of talks, reflecting hundreds of hours of prayerful contemplation and effort. I'm always happy to share, and I hope those who read this book will find enjoyment and "food for thought."

Whenever I've been asked to teach, to speak, I've done my best to seek heavenly help in preparing both the material and myself. I feel deeply that the *real* teacher is the Holy Ghost, and so I earnestly seek His guidance when I'm invited to teach. It is my hope that as you read you'll seek this same guidance, so that you'll receive more than I knew how to say or write.

One thing I've tried to do is select a variety of topics so that the book doesn't read like "same old, same old." You may be one of the people to whom I've told the story of a woman who came up to me after I'd given a talk somewhere, and she made me nervous because (a) she looked "ticked off," and (b) she was in my personal space (ha!) . . . in my face. She said pointedly, "I've heard that talk before." Not knowing quite how to respond, I just said, "Me too."

So you may read something you've heard before. That thought gives me a chance to share something President Gordon B. Hinckley said in general conference in October 2007: "My brothers and sisters, we live with an interesting phenomenon. A soloist sings the same song again and again. An orchestra repeats the same music. But a speaker is expected to come up with something new every time he speaks" (*Ensign,* November 2007, 83).

I love that quote. I'm pretty sure I'll be using it quite a bit for the rest of my life.

I'm so grateful to the excellent team at Deseret Book, particularly Jana Erickson and Emily Watts. These two friends and all who work with them are over-the-top wonderful. They take a bunch of printed, drafty pages and make them beautiful. I thank each one of them very sincerely.

Donations from the sales of this particular book will go to the LDS Church's Missionary Fund. I'm hoping my little contribution will help with the teaching and preaching of truth throughout the world. Thanks for helping.

Somebody

I was thinking that somewhere in this big world this morning, a woman is praying for her mother, who's now living in an assisted care place and spends so much time alone. She's praying that SOMEBODY will notice her mother, will touch her, be kind to her, make sure she's all right.

And somewhere in the world there's a father whose boy is going to start in the "regular" school class next week after being in special ed for several years. Oh, how he's hoping that SOMEBODY will reach out to his little boy and build trust and friendship with him.

There's a daughter somewhere who knows her dad should quit driving, but she hasn't been able to stop him yet. He's careful and doesn't go far from home, but he drives so slowly. And she's hoping that SOMEBODY will be patient with him as he's holding on tightly to one of his last sources of independence.

In an apartment building there's an older woman living alone who doesn't have any family living nearby, and it's too cold and snowy for her to go out much. She's wishing SOMEBODY would stop by to visit with her and perhaps help her with a couple of things she hasn't been able to do.

In a home not too far away there's a wonderful man caring for his wife who has Alzheimer's, and it's almost to the point where he can't do it alone anymore. He'd love to have SOMEBODY come by and help him make some extremely difficult decisions.

There's a single mom in the neighborhood who's feeling completely overwhelmed with trying to put together a wonderful Christmas for her children, not knowing how she's going to pay for it all along with the many regular bills. She's desperate for SOMEBODY to help in some way but doesn't know whom to ask and is not even quite sure what she needs.

Well, I didn't mean to have quite that many examples, but I hope you get the idea. I want to be SOMEBODY. I think you know what I mean—what that feeling is like. We all have times, don't we, of wanting to be more aware of those who are around us, wanting to see if we can do little things (or even sometimes big things) to make a difference.

I want to tell you a true story about Pam, Natalie, and Leanne. I like true stories best, because you don't have to make anything up.

I'll start with Pam. She's Natalie's incredible mother. I'll let her tell her story herself:

"Natalie was born with lots of medical complications. She cannot walk, talk, sit up, crawl, or move herself. Although she had these problems, she had always been healthy in the sense that she never got sick.

"Unfortunately, in December of 2005 she began to have health problems. She ended up being in the hospital for 150 days during the next one and a half years. She received twelve blood transfusions and multiple surgeries.

"In August of 2006, when Natalie was seven, we took her into the ER because of respiratory distress. Due to a hiatal hernia, gastric acid from the stomach was shooting up the esophagus. During the night, she inhaled some of this acid. She stopped breathing and had to be resuscitated. Two surgeries later, Natalie had an artificial hiatus and was no longer able to eat on her own and couldn't tolerate any food by mouth. She began to receive nourishment through a feeding tube.

3

"With the help of a physician who specialized in nutrition for neurologically impaired children, a special diet was created. The 'recipe' was pretty specific and complicated. I had to drive all over the place to get all the organic ingredients and then go through a process of cooking, grinding, and blending the food to a consistency fine enough to go through Natalie's feeding tube pump without clogging anything.

"During this time, I had visited Temple Square during a three-hour stopover in Salt Lake City, Utah. I had a lot of questions, and the tour guide asked if I'd like to have someone come to my home in California and answer these and other questions.

"Missionaries stopped by, and they helped me become acquainted with my neighbor, Leanne. I didn't know her very well; but when we talked I told her what was going on with Natalie. She immediately asked if there was anything she could do to help. I politely refused—I don't feel comfortable inconveniencing people. But Leanne said, 'Why don't I come over right now, and you can show me how to make the food for Natalie, and then I'll make it for you.' And she did. A woman I barely knew had come to help.

"She proceeded to take over the entire task—doing

the shopping, cooking the food, grinding it up, and then blending it until it was of such a fine consistency that it would go through the feeding tube without trouble—no small task! She spent a lot of time trying to figure out the best way to do it, and bought an expensive blender that could 'blend' the cooked beef to the finest texture. She also bought a manual grinder to get the food to an even finer consistency.

"Leanne spent hours and hours making Natalie's food each week, and carefully packaged it up so that we could track the calories she was getting. She has done more for me than any other friend I've had, and I will always remember what she did for Natalie and me. It made such a difference for us during that hard time."

Now let's hear from the neighbor, Leanne.

"In the fall of 2006, I reintroduced myself to my neighbor, Pam, a single mother of five, at the invitation of our missionaries. They had followed up on a request made by Pam at Temple Square. I invited her to attend church meetings and activities with me. She wasn't able to go and eventually let me know what was happening with her youngest daughter, Natalie.

"Pam explained the care Natalie needed, with daily feeding, bathing, therapy, etc. With her other children and the work she needed to do to support her family, Pam had a full plate. I could quickly see how devoted she was to Natalie. It became easy for us to talk, as we both had several children and many things in common.

"I soon realized that Pam needed somebody who could and would lift even a small part of the burden she had been trying to carry herself. Natalie was being fed canned protein drinks through a feeding tube and was not doing well on this diet.

"Then Pam got in touch with a doctor back East who suggested a diet that began working wonders for Natalie. She was gaining weight and wasn't in constant pain any longer. But the ingredients were hard to find, and they had to be cooked very slowly at a low temperature to get them soft enough to 'fall apart' and blend to a fine consistency. Then the ingredients had to be put through a very fine sieve or strainer.

"Pam was having to leave Natalie at the hospital to drive to every health food store in the area, then go home to prepare the food and take it back to the hospital.

"One day while talking to her I felt prompted to ask, 'What can I do to help?' Pam couldn't come up with anything, so I just told her I was going to come over and learn how to make the food. That's all it took. Pam showed me how, and for a couple of months I made Natalie's food. I did this until Natalie finally came home from the hospital and was doing better, and Pam felt like she could handle everything herself."

This is where you want Paul Harvey to come in and tell you "the rest of the story." He's not here, so I hope I can do an adequate job.

Natalie is doing much better these days, although she still faces a lot of challenges in her young life. She has a wonderful mother looking out for her, a mother who recently married again and is very happy. Pam and Leanne have become good friends and are keeping in touch.

One thing that impressed me in Pam's account was this: "What stood out most in my mind was that the Mormons walk their walk. I have plenty of religious friends who have said that they would pray for me, but it was Leanne, a woman I barely knew, who actually went way out of her way and made a significant difference for us."

She was SOMEBODY.

You've had your own sweet experiences, haven't you? I hope you've written them down (as President Henry B.

Eyring has encouraged us to do) so that they might become a source of inspiration and blessing to others.

I'm convinced that as we open our hearts to heavenly influences, the SOMEBODY who is the Father of us all will give us wonderful (and sometimes challenging) chances to be a blessing to others.

Today and every day, let's be SOMEBODY.

The Bucket and the Dipper

Several years ago I came across a funny, clever thought about buckets and dippers, and I wish I knew who first came up with it, because I'd love to tell them thank you for the fun I've had in playing with this idea. I think some good lessons are taught. Here is my most recent version:

Once upon a time in the long, long ago, it was discovered that everyone has a bucket. No kidding. This bucket is a kind of vessel that can be filled . . . even to overflowing.

The things in the bucket include stuff like peace, comfort, love, joy, strength, and such. And the fuller it is, the easier it is to share what's in your bucket with others.

Due to a kind PIC (Person In Charge), we get to help fill each other's buckets. Isn't that great! And there are a lot of wonderful ways we can do that.

For example, we can say "Good morning!" when we

see each other. That's a great way to make a little donation in someone else's bucket. You can double the contribution by adding the person's name, and triple it with a genuine smile.

Other things that can fill up another's bucket are hugs, listening, sincere praise, pointing out strengths, being sensitive to needs (and doing something about them when you can), cheerfulness, honesty, patience (almost sounds like a description of charity, the pure love of Christ, when you think about it).

Anyway, one of the things we all ought to spend time doing forever is helping to fill others' buckets.

Now, it must needs be, so they say, that there is opposition in all things. And so, just as we each have a bucket, we each have a dipper. Yup. And sometimes, other people can get their dippers in your bucket! It's been known to happen!

Just imagine that we're going out to eat with some of our friends. First-class restaurant—nice tablecloth, beautiful silverware, flowers, and so on. There's soft music, the place is lovely, the service outstanding.

I've just had a bath, and I'm feeling good. I am sitting at the table visiting, and I accidentally knock over my glass of V-8 juice. Big red spot. I am so embarrassed. I am turning redder than I'm usually red.

The juice just keeps crawling across the table right toward our host, the one who invited us to this classy restaurant. It's like a flood! It won't stop!

And then, finally, it does it: It dribbles on her! She jumps a little, but is being nice even though it's wet and gooey. And then my neighbor, my so-called friend, old "bright eyes" down the table a little, looks up and says, "You spilled your juice."

She got her dipper in my bucket!

Tell me how old you have to be to know you've made a mistake! Can you remember ever sitting down to breakfast or lunch with your family and your little brother spilled his milk? And about thirty-five people (it seemed) said, "You spilled your milk!"

All those great big dippers in that tiny little bucket. . . .

Have you noticed that there are times when you can't seem to help it, when you're getting your dipper in others' buckets like crazy, and you just can't stop? And have you ever noticed that when you get your dipper in somebody's bucket, you're usually pointing out something *wrong* with them? This is not good. No, this is not good at all.

You tell your sister she's got wrinkles in her nylons . . . and she hasn't got 'em on yet.

You tell someone she's moody and then you find out she has a toothache or she got a sad letter or she lost her MP3 player.

You tell someone there's a spot on his face and then find out your glasses are dirty.

You've got your dipper in someone else's bucket!

It might feel good, sort of, when you first shove your dipper into someone's bucket—but after a while it doesn't feel good anymore. You know that, don't you? I do too.

Do you know what a "dip-in" is? It's not exactly like a drive-in or a sit-in. It's when several people get together and just dip someone good!

Next time you realize that's happening, point it out—stop it! Shout, "Hey, we've all got our dippers in that bucket! Let's fill it instead of emptying it!"

Have you ever noticed that when your bucket is low, or empty—when you need most to have someone put something in it—that is when you tend to push people away? You might even put a lock on the lid on your bucket, a sure sign that you don't want anyone putting anything in, even if they're trying their best to help.

Sometimes you say to yourself, "Self, she's got a *lid* on her bucket!" Or you may ask, "Hey, does anyone know where I can buy a lid for my bucket? There are a lot of *dips* around this place!"

You may feel like slamming the lid on someone's dipper. "I'll show her!" You hope to at least bend it, if not break it. "You'll do no more dipping today, Cruella!"

Some of you may even think you don't *have* a bucket! Or you may feel that your bucket's been shot full of holes.

Or on some days you might just feel like you want to "kick the bucket"! Excuse me?

Well, for *sure* we're just not the same when our buckets are empty, and that's all there is to it.

AND we're not the same when we're dipping instead of filling, and that's all there is to that, too! If you really want to be happy, keep your dipper out of others' buckets.

FILL someone's bucket today—and you'll discover yours is getting fuller too. Full to overflowing—you'll have so much, much more to share. It really could be that way. It really *can* be that way.

Let's do the best we can to love one another, enrich and lift, bless and fill.

Peace amidst Suffering

For many, many years, I've thought and wondered a lot about the topic of peace amidst suffering. Maybe you have too.

I used to think of it as something more like "peace despite suffering." But the more I pondered and observed, the more I realized that we experience peace *with* our suffering, in the *midst* of our suffering. I'd like to share some thoughts about why I feel this way.

I'm convinced that we're not going to get through this life without suffering. But I'm also convinced that as we stay close to our Heavenly Father, our Savior, and the Holy Ghost, we will also not have to go through this life without peace—genuine, sweet, comforting *peace.*

What *is* suffering? Usually it's tied to experiences that are painful or unpleasant. It seems generally to require holding on, waiting patiently, and enduring. To suffer also means to allow—to submit.

I think there is no one who has been spared from suffering personally, or from watching others suffer.

What, then, is peace? Peace is knowing that the One in charge of *everything* is our Father, and that He not only *knows* everything, He *understands,* and that His Plan is the Great Plan of Happiness! Peace is a critical ingredient of happiness.

There are examples throughout the scriptures of Heavenly Father's children experiencing peace amidst suffering.

In Alma 1:28, it is recorded that the people of God were being persecuted terribly. Persecution was being *heaped* upon them! But they kept the commandments and established a Zion society right in the midst of their adversity and suffering. "And thus they did establish the affairs of the church; and thus they began to have continual peace again, notwithstanding all their persecutions."

Hang on to that idea in your darkest, hardest hours—hang on to the fact that they did it. They experienced peace and joy amidst suffering!

Another example, one I know you're familiar with, was when Alma Senior and the people whom he baptized at the waters of Mormon (Mosiah 18) were in captivity, being persecuted by the priests of King Noah (a group to which Alma had belonged before he came to his senses).

I've selected just a few excerpts from their story in Mosiah 23–24. Watch for some wonderful lessons.

Alma told the people of his sore repentance and conversion, including this thought: "*After much tribulation,* the Lord did hear my cries, and did answer my prayers" (23:10; emphasis added).

Alma and his people settled in the land of Helam, and they prospered exceedingly, but then look what happened: "Nevertheless the Lord seeth fit to chasten his people; yea, he trieth their patience and their faith. Nevertheless—whosoever putteth his trust in him the same shall be lifted up at the last day" (23:21–22). (Do you ever wish that being "lifted up" could happen a day or two *before* the "last day"?)

The believers were put into captivity by the Lamanites, with the former priests of king Noah to guard them, and life became extremely difficult. "And it came to pass that so great were their afflictions that they began to cry mightily to God" (24:10).

That made Amulon, who had authority over Alma and his people, very mad. He told the guards to kill anyone caught praying! So they "did not raise their voices to the Lord their God, but did pour out their hearts to him; and he did know the thoughts of their hearts" (24:12).

Then the voice of the Lord came to them *in their afflictions.* He told them to be comforted because He would deliver them out of bondage. And He shared a sweet, tender message with them. Put *yourself* in these verses if you can, will you? Try applying this perspective to some of the difficult things you might be experiencing:

"I will also ease the burdens which are put upon your shoulders, that even you cannot feel them upon your backs, even while you are in bondage [*before* they were delivered]; and this will I do that ye may stand as witnesses for me hereafter, and that ye may know of a surety that I, the Lord God, do visit my people in their afflictions.

"And now it came to pass that the burdens . . . were made light; yea, the Lord did strengthen them that they could bear up their burdens with ease, and they did submit cheerfully and with patience to all the will of the Lord" (24:14–15).

Imagine that! Have you had any experience that helps you understand even a little bit what this must have been like? I am awed at the thought that many who have been visited by God in their afflictions may be called upon to stand as witnesses of it!

One more example of peace amidst suffering, this one from Liberty Jail and the experience of the Prophet Joseph Smith. He was languishing in jail. He had poured out his heart and feelings to his Heavenly Father, beginning with "O God, where art thou?" Among many other comforting things, the Lord answered: "My son, peace be unto thy soul; thine adversity and thine afflictions shall be but a small moment; and then, if thou endure it well, God shall exalt thee on high" (D&C 121:7–8).

I think that's what God asks of us: "My daughter, peace be unto thy soul. I know what you're going through. Endure it well."

Have you ever thought that God expects too much of us? Haven't there been a few days in your life when you've come close to feeling that He's asked too much of you, that you can't cope with it all?

Elder Bruce R. McConkie reminded us that our trials are not yet over: "Nor are the days of our greatest sorrows and our deepest sufferings all behind us. They too lie ahead. We shall yet face greater perils, we shall yet be tested with more severe trials, and we shall yet weep more tears of sorrow than we have ever before known" (*Ensign,* May 1980, 71).

Does that frighten you, or make you feel unsettled? Have you purchased extra insurance and Kleenex?

No one needs to be reminded, I think, of the suffering going on in this world. Much of it is in faraway places with strange-sounding names, and it's horrific. There is so much of illness, injustice, insensitivity, poverty, loneliness, helplessness, estrangement from loved ones, physical and emotional abuse, loss of hope, disappointment, broken hearts and spirits, being misrepresented or misquoted or misunderstood.

But there is suffering closer, in your own country, your own village, and likely even your own home and your own heart. What are *your* deep waters and fiery trials? What are *you* going through at this time in your life?

When I thought of sharing some of my own experiences, it made me uncomfortable. I thought, "Well, I've not really suffered anything worth mentioning." I haven't had many of the same experiences you've had. But there *are* some things in my life that have been difficult for me, and that I might remember as having involved some degree of suffering.

For example, I thought for sure I would be married

and have children, and it's hard knowing that just has not happened for me.

One Sunday as my mother and I were coming out of sacrament meeting and I was helping her into the car, she said something like, "One of these days *you'll* be old, and then you'll know how I feel." And I responded (without really thinking about it first), "I know. And when that day comes, oh how I wish I could have a daughter like me." It caught us both off guard, and we cried together.

I've had other experiences when it *seemed* like I was suffering, at least some of the time.

Have you ever been in a situation where you wanted to give all you had and yet you couldn't because of some limitations? That happened to me when I was in Nigeria, West Africa, to help with a child health project. I'll tell you right up front that I was *not* a visual aid for good health.

I felt reluctant to say yes to this assignment, because I know I don't get along well in certain climates. It so happens that I have a hard time in humid places. And when you picture this spot in Nigeria where I'd been asked to go, think African rain forest. Think over-the-top humidity.

When my prayers about going to Africa were

answered—"Yes, I want you to go"—I thought that meant I would be *well*. I was wrong. It seemed like I became sick almost immediately. And I was sick the whole time I was there. My asthma made it impossible for me to sleep or rest well. Asthma is frightening—if you've had it, you know what I mean.

There never was a day when I could breathe deeply and freely. My resistance was "below zero." I've sometimes said with a smile that "the people made me sick!" I'd hug and kiss the children, and within hours, it seemed, I would get whatever bugs they had.

I didn't like murmuring, so I turned my pain inward. I never felt mad at God. I was puzzled and curious, but not mad. I'd had enough other experiences in my life to know that He hadn't planned something to "get back at me," or whatever. I knew that something good had to come of all this, so, although I *was* frustrated, it was mostly at my own inability to have what it took to get well and stay well.

It was hard to keep my spirits up, especially in a situation where living was difficult even on the best days. Whether it was purifying our water, washing our clothes or dishes, keeping the house clean, or doing what we had come to do—the child health project—it all was much harder for me because of my poor health.

I got discouraged because I had received several very special priesthood blessings, and I felt I lacked the faith to help them "come true."

One day near Thanksgiving I wrote a short but revealing sentence in my journal: "Sometimes I really wonder if I'll ever in my whole life feel strong and healthy again."

Then came Tuesday, January 8, 1985. My incredible companion, Ann, who would literally save my life a few days later, had gone to another village with the couple missionaries. They were gone the whole day.

It was an unusual, unforgettable day for me. I had a long, long talk with Heavenly Father. I cried a lot, because I didn't want Him to think that I was complaining— that I was mad at Him or felt like He was the cause of everything I was going through. But I felt convinced that *He had asked me to come.* And I wondered why.

My "why" question was not, "Why do I have to suffer?" It wasn't like I felt like a martyr or something. But I did wonder what this experience meant for me and what I was supposed to do with it and about it.

This was one of the most sacred and important days

of the whole experience. I was at a low ebb, but I wasn't bitter. If I'd been bitter or angry, I know that what happened would not have occurred. I just needed to talk to Him. I needed Him to tell me that He knew where I was, and that *He* knew why, even if I didn't.

And so, on that day alone, I wasn't alone at all. I was closer to my Heavenly Father than I've been very many times in my life. I sat at the window in the living room of what Ann and I called "The Palace," our home, and I held onto the bars on the window and wept. (I can't help but tell you that it's hard to cry when you have asthma!)

I asked, "What do You want from me?" That may sound like a sarcastic or biting question, but I asked it softly and humbly. I *knew* that He had not asked me to come to such a place for no reason.

I suppose Heavenly Father could have said something like, "Oh, it's really nothing—what you've been through—when compared to what my Son and Joseph Smith and millions and billions of others have experienced." But He didn't.

What He whispered to me was so completely comforting and personal that the feeling remains with me today. First, He put the following thought into my soul: "I will make it up to you." Those are my words, not His.

I don't remember exactly what I "heard" inside of me, but that's what it meant in my "earthling" language: "I will make it up to you."

I told Him that wasn't what I wanted or needed, but He wouldn't take it back. It was a definite, strong impression and it wouldn't go away.

And then we had a long visit about what He wanted me to do. He asked if I had any idea of how much I would have learned and understood if I had felt completely healthy the whole time I was there. I told Him I likely would have missed *much.* He agreed. He gave me an indication that some of my most important lessons might still be coming.

I didn't ask Him how long He wanted me to stay there. It wasn't one of those times when I was in a hurry for *anything.* I wanted everything to go very slowly so that I could take it all in the best I could. I wanted to *remember* this most significant day and time in my life. I wanted to have it sink deep into my soul and be there forever. I felt so personally and sweetly attended to during that time. It may be that there were others who helped to comfort and teach me on that unusual day (see D&C 84:88).

I don't think I could ever do a very good job of

sharing with you all that I felt on that day, but it was so sweet amidst all the awfulness that I let Him know I would go on and on if He asked me to—that I would stay as long as He wanted. I pray that I will never forget that day in Africa when He *visited me*. . . .

How I wish I could share *your* stories—that I could know something about *your* heavy burdens and trials. Do you get feeling overwhelmed? Tired? Sometimes frightened? Does it sometimes catch you off guard that you feel so discouraged? Do you wonder why some of your prayers aren't answered in the way you had hoped? Has it been a long time since any of your fondest dreams have come true? Do you ever feel lonely? Do you have bad habits that you just can't seem to break? Have you lost a child or another loved one? Have you been treated with unkindness or cruelty? Do the days go by too quickly . . . or too slowly? Has someone betrayed you—broken your heart and your trust? Are you worn out? Deeply in debt? Weary? All of the above?

Is it really possible for us to have peace amidst suffering? What did the Savior say? "Peace I leave with you, my peace I give unto you: not as the world giveth, give I unto you. Let not your heart be troubled, neither let it be afraid" (John 14:27).

The answer is YES! We *can* experience peace amidst suffering, because the Prince of Peace said so!

Jesus is described as a man of sorrows, and acquainted with grief. Having experienced *our* suffering, He said: "Come unto me, all ye that labour and are heavy laden, and I will give you rest. Take my yoke upon you, and learn of me; for I am meek and lowly in heart: and ye shall find rest unto your souls. For my yoke is easy, and my burden is light" (Matthew 11:28–30).

He didn't promise a shortcut to heaven or a life free of adversity . . . but *rest*—rest to our souls.

Through afflictions, we learn to trust the Lord completely, knowing that whatever happens, all eventually will be right. He will "make it up" to us. Everything will be sorted out, everything will be fair, wrongs will be righted, tears will be wiped away, no one will be hungry or thirsty or naked or sick or imprisoned or frightened or lonely or hurting.

Through all that is difficult in life, the gospel of Jesus Christ offers peace and comfort. Sweet is the peace the gospel brings.

Finding Purpose in Our Pain

In the previous chapter, we explored the possibility that we could find peace even in the middle of our sufferings. I'd like to take that a step further in this chapter. I believe we can find not just *peace* but *purpose* in the suffering we experience in mortality.

I want you to think of an experience that was extremely difficult for you—one of the hardest you've ever had to face. (Maybe you're going through it right now.)

Now I want to ask you a question about your adversity, your suffering: What have you learned from your experiences? Have you learned compassion? Is your heart more tender? Do you judge others less quickly and harshly?

Our suffering helps to purify and sanctify us. Maybe we shouldn't try to get rid of everything so quickly, without or before *learning.* President Spencer W. Kimball taught

27

that if we close the doors upon sorrow, distress, and anguish in our lives, "we might be evicting our greatest friends and benefactors. Suffering can make saints of people as they learn patience, long-suffering, and self-mastery. The sufferings of our Savior were part of his education" (*Teachings of Spencer W. Kimball* [Bookcraft, 1982], 168).

And from the Apostle Paul: "We glory in tribulations also: knowing that tribulation worketh patience; and patience, experience; and experience, hope: and hope maketh not ashamed; because the love of God is shed abroad in our hearts by the Holy Ghost which is given unto us" (Romans 5:3–5). Can you recognize times when your tribulations led you to patience and hope?

President Brigham Young experienced a fair amount of adversity and suffering. His words are worth pondering:

"God never bestows upon His people, or upon an individual, superior blessings without a severe trial to prove them, to prove that individual, or that people, to see whether they will keep their covenants with Him, and keep in remembrance what He has shown them. Then the greater the vision, the greater the display of the power of the enemy" (*Journal of Discourses* [26 vols., Latter-day Saints Book Depot, 1854–86], 3:206).

"Every trial and experience you have passed through is necessary for your salvation" (*Journal of Discourses,* 8:150).

"The people of the Most High God must be tried. . . . I think there is a prospect for the Saints to have all the trials they wish for, or can desire" (*Journal of Discourses,* 4:369).

Two verses in one of our hymns, "How Firm a Foundation," help me to know that there is purpose in all that we experience of "hard times":

> *When through the deep waters I call thee to go,*
> *The rivers of sorrow shall not thee o'erflow,*
> *For I will be with thee, thy troubles to bless,*
> *And sanctify to thee thy deepest distress.*
>
> *When through fiery trials thy pathway shall lie,*
> *My grace, all sufficient, shall be thy supply.*
> *The flame shall not hurt thee; I only design*
> *Thy dross to consume and thy gold to refine.*
> (Hymns, *no. 85)*

Can you see that to sanctify and purify us, our Heavenly Father designs experiences that will help us

29

become more like Him—more pure and holy—more "fit for the kingdom"?

But we don't always feel that way, do we? How do we keep from becoming bitter or angry or separated from God if we feel that something is unjust or unfair? Sometimes when I sit in a meeting where testimonies are being shared about miracles, I know there are people sitting in that chapel who are suffering *so deeply* because they didn't have the miracle they'd hoped for. . . .

I'm thinking of two prophets in the Book of Mormon. Alma Senior had a son who was apparently very wicked and anti-Church. He went about with his friends trying to destroy all that his father was doing. Alma Senior fasted and prayed long and hard for his son, Alma Junior. (So did his mother, I'm sure.) You know the story—Alma Junior and his friends were visited by an angel in an experience that changed their hearts and their lives. They became some of the most powerful missionaries in history. And Alma Junior became a great prophet and chief judge.

Lehi's eldest son, Laman, became anti-Church and anti-father and even sought to murder his father and his brother Nephi. *His* visit from an angel doesn't seem to have had much lasting effect on him.

Both prophets prayed and fasted for their sons and did everything they could think of to persuade them to believe in Christ and follow Heavenly Father's plan. Was Alma Senior more faithful than Lehi? Was he more obedient, more worthy? Did God love him more? Did he pray with greater faith? It makes me weep to even *think* of such questions.

President Spencer W. Kimball reminded us that "Prayers are not always answered as we wish them to be. Even the Redeemer's prayer in Gethsemane was answered in the negative" (*Teachings of Spencer W. Kimball,* 124).

It takes *complete trust* in our Heavenly Father to be able to leave things in His loving hands. Has it ever been hard for you to say and *mean* these words: "Thy will be done"? (Some say, "For dumb! That cancels out your prayer!")

As we respond with faith and patience to adversity and suffering, we become stronger, sweeter, and increasingly gentle and kind. Our feelings about the Savior are deeper. Our communication with our Heavenly Father is so much more meaningful and real. We can feel Him and His Son and the Comforter helping us to endure.

President Marion G. Romney quoted this statement from Joseph Smith: "Men have to suffer that they may come upon Mount Zion and be exalted above the heavens" (*History of the Church* [6 vols. Deseret Book, 1948], 5:556). President Romney then said: "This does not mean that we crave suffering. We avoid all we can. However, we now know, and we all knew when we elected to come into mortality, that we would here be proved in the 'crucible' of adversity and affliction" (*Look to God and Live* [Deseret Book, 1973], 241–42).

God will have a tried and proven people, a pure people.

So, what can we do with these trials that are part of our learning process? Or, if things are "slow" for us right now in the adversity department, how can we help others get through *their* difficulties?

We read in Romans 12:15: "Rejoice with them that do rejoice, and weep with them that weep." Sometimes the suffering we feel as we seek to help lift another's burdens, to mourn with each other and comfort one another, is the most exquisite and painful. The suffering of our souls is no small thing. We may wish from the center of our heart to reach out to others, even those we don't know—we just see them on the news or hear about their situation. They live across oceans and across the street . . . and sometimes they're across the room. They are hungry, thirsty, sick, naked, imprisoned, homeless, hopeless. They are dealing with abject poverty, disease, floods, fires, war, ignorance, death . . . and we *can* help!

One person can't solve all the problems of the world. One person can't even solve all the problems in his or her own nation, village, neighborhood, or family.

But one person can visit another person. One willing covenant woman can reach out and lighten another's burden. One kind soul can call another, can write a note, can pray with all her heart, can share hope. One of the ways in which we are blessed, comforted, and protected is through each other's consecrated service.

Are there some things we might do that *aren't* helpful when others are hurting? What are some things we perhaps *shouldn't* do as we face adversity and suffering, or as we try to help others through their hard times?

It doesn't seem very helpful to say something like, "Oh, I know *exactly* how you feel . . ." "I know *just* what you mean!" We likely don't.

Can we be more honest? "I'm not sure I understand, but I'm *so sorry.*" Weep with those who weep, and just listen.

Sometimes we try to talk people *out* of a difficulty instead of helping them *through* it. What did Paul mean when he taught us that if "one member suffer, all the members suffer with it"? (1 Corinthians 12:26). When you lighten another's burdens, when you mourn with those that mourn, when you are suffering with one of the members who suffers, you *feel* it. You do suffer with them.

We seem to want a quick cure from every single ounce of suffering or adversity that comes our way. Greeting cards often say, "Get well soon." What other kinds of messages might we share with someone who's suffering? "Hope the learning and growing isn't *too* painful." "May your deep water and fiery trials not be more than you can handle." "I hope you'll let me travel part of the journey with you." "May you feel comforted in this time of learning and refining." "Can I help in any way?" "I know our Heavenly Father is aware of you and feel that He is weeping with you."

Another thing we probably need to avoid is competing for "worst trial." Have you ever seen people compare their suffering to see if they can "top" (or "bottom") everyone else because theirs is so much more spectacular or difficult.

"Oh, you think *that's* bad . . ."

"My kidney stone was a much nicer shape than yours!"

"My tonsils were a *lot* worse than that! Want to see the picture?"

"I was in labor for forty days and forty nights!"

"My root canal went clear to my collarbone!"

Let's not discount *anything* that is heavy for anyone else to bear, just because it doesn't seem to be as awful as what we have experienced.

If we're ever tempted to try to "top" someone in their suffering, thinking it's not much compared to what *we've* been through (or are going through), maybe we could just remember that someday we will see the Savior again, and there will be no way we can even approach an adequate, accurate understanding of what *He* has suffered *for us.*

President Marion G. Romney reminded us that "The Father's plan for proving his children did not exempt the Savior himself. The suffering he [endured] . . . equaled the combined suffering of all men. Eighteen hundred years after he had endured it, he spoke of it as being so intense that it 'caused myself, even God, the greatest of all, to tremble because of pain, and to bleed at every pore, and to suffer both body and spirit—and would that

I might not drink the bitter cup, and shrink—Nevertheless, [he concluded] glory be to the Father, and I partook and finished my preparations unto the children of men.' (D&C 19:18–19)" (*Look to God and Live,* 242).

Maybe one of the most important lessons we learn from our own adversity, our own trials and suffering, is a deeper appreciation and love for our Savior. How can we help but think of His infinite sacrifice, and the fact that He *is* our Redeemer and Savior, and that He *can* heal us, make us whole, and bring us Home.

Don't ever quit pouring out your heart to your Heavenly Father. Please don't ever doubt His love for you. You are His child.

Don't worry or doubt or fear—your Father loves you *dearly* and will never forget or forsake you. From the final verse of "How Firm a Foundation" comes this assurance:

> *The soul that on Jesus hath leaned for repose*
> *I will not, I cannot, desert to his foes;*
> *That soul, though all hell should endeavor to shake,*
> *I'll never, no never, no never forsake!*
>   (Hymns, *no. 85)*

Suffering can be holy and sacred. Suffer well, knowing you're never alone. May we feel that peace and hope He has made possible, even in the midst of our suffering.

The Rabbit Judge

One wonderful day at the Missionary Training Center I had the privilege of greeting some senior missionaries on their very first day. Oh, I know what they were feeling! We gathered in one of the classrooms and I shared some information that I hoped would be helpful in the first few hours and days of their adventure.

One couple began to capture my attention. I noticed that they sat in the back corner, and that they seemed uncomfortable. The brother, for example, was "fighting" with his collar and tie, as if he weren't accustomed to wearing them. My feelings became increasingly tender as I watched them during my short presentation.

At one point I was telling the missionaries that when they came to their first meeting with the mission president later in the day they should bring their scriptures. When our brief orientation ended, this couple waited until others had left the room, and then they approached me and asked, "Which scriptures should we take to that meeting?"

I remember clearly how aware I was of pleading with Heavenly Father to guide me to be *helpful* and *gentle* at this moment of worry and awkwardness for this wonderful couple.

I said, "Well, let's see what you have there." They held out a brand spankin' new quadruple combination—the four Standard Works in one volume—in "mint condition." I thought perhaps it had been a gift from their children or some good friends or neighbors. I said, "These will be exactly what you need." We visited for a few more minutes, and then they left.

I found myself watching out for this couple, whom I'll call Elder and Sister Dowdle. I wanted to make sure they were all right. I alerted those with whom I worked to the need for support and encouragement.

One morning a few days after they arrived, Elder and Sister Dowdle were in a class I was teaching. I don't remember exactly what the topic was, but of course I would have used some illustrations from others' experiences to let the missionaries know what kinds of activities might be part of their missions.

Once again, Elder and Sister Dowdle stayed after

others had left. He had his suit jacket off this day and was fiddling with his suspenders as he tried to tell me what was on his mind. His dear wife explained sweetly, "He has a hard time telling what he's feeling."

And then the dam broke, and the tears came, and he blurted out a few things like, "I can't *do* this! I don't *know* anything! I'll *never* be able to be a missionary!"

His wife held onto his arm and said to me, "He's really a good man—he's just nervous about this . . . and I am too."

A phrase I love is "my heart went out to him." We use that often as we speak to each other of such sacred moments. Here were two great souls who were frightened of a new calling—of doing something they had never done before. And my heart *did* go out to them, and particularly to him.

"Elder Dowdle," I said, "tell me about yourself. What are some of the things you've done in your life?"

He couldn't talk. He was trying not to cry. But his wife said proudly, "He's a rabbit judge!"

For the first time in my life, I was standing face-to-face with a rabbit judge! I told him that: "I have never in my whole life met a genuine rabbit judge! What do you do?" He began to tell me what it took to be a rabbit judge. Slowly but surely some confidence crept into his voice and his posture. I think this man knew every rabbit between Ely and Elko!

We visited for quite a while, and I tried to say things that I really meant, things that might in some way help Elder and Sister Dowdle to know that the Lord was aware of all their life's experience, and would help them to love and comfort and strengthen others.

They were *much* on my mind after that, and soon I had an idea that wouldn't leave. It occurred to me that many of the senior missionaries were going to places where they might need to know something about rabbits. I went to ask as many as I could find, explaining just enough so they "caught on." *Every single one* wanted to know more about rabbits!

I then went to Elder Dowdle and asked if he would be willing to take about an hour and teach the rest of us something about rabbits—especially about raising them for meat, for a good source of protein. He grinned and asked if I was serious. I assured him I was.

We set it up in one of the classrooms, and we gathered and watched a miracle. As he began to share what he knew so well, we learned *so much!* Questions were specific and meaningful, and he could answer with ease and confidence.

After that, it was easy for all of us to treat Elder Dowdle with the respect he deserved. It changed not just him but the rest of us too.

Every single person I have ever met in my life has had something important to teach me. Has it been the same for you? I regret that I have not always given every person a chance to teach me—to enrich me. But when I've done so, I've been rewarded in such unusually wonderful ways!

An experience like this is not just about helping others be and feel successful—it's *recognizing* what they know and can share. My prayer is that Heavenly Father will touch my eyes that I may see, and help my heart to be aware of what's going on around me. I hope we might always be led to those who might need some attention, some kindness, some love . . . some opportunity.

Friendship

Do you remember your first friend? How old were you at the time, and where did you live? What were some of your favorite things to do with your friends when you were a child?

I'm still close to the first friend I remember having. I was three years old, and our family had moved from California to Cedar City in Southern Utah. The Palmers lived across the street and up a few houses. Zonie and I became friends immediately and have remained friends for all the years that have followed.

We'd sleep out on her lawn, looking at all the stars (there were more back then) and finding one that we knew no one else had ever, *ever* seen, and we'd call it our special star. We kept it a secret from all but our closest friends.

Having friends has been an important blessing to me my whole life. I think most people feel the same way.

I love what the Lord said to Joseph Smith when Joseph was in Liberty Jail: "Thy friends do stand by thee . . . with warm hearts and friendly hands" (D&C 121:9). I've thought so many times about what a difference it made for him to have some of his best friends be members of his own family, including his wonderful parents. And his brothers, especially Hyrum, who was to Joseph as Jonathan was to David as recorded in the Old Testament (see *History of the Church,* 5:107–8). These brothers had a sacred bond of genuine friendship, unselfish and tender—a friendship of that pure quality of which there are but few instances on record. Hyrum watched tenderly over Joseph. He was a peacemaker and was faithful to the death. "In life they were not divided, and in death they were not separated!" (D&C 135:3).

The Prophet Joseph Smith was an extraordinary friend to others. He taught that "Friendship is one of the grand fundamental principles of 'Mormonism'; . . . friendship is like Brother Turley in his blacksmith shop welding iron to iron; it unites the human family with its happy influence" (*History of the Church,* 5:517).

In a letter to his dear wife Emma in the midst of their many trials, Joseph wrote: "Oh my affectionate Emma, I want you to remember that I am a true and faithful friend to you and the children, forever" (Dean C. Jessee, ed., *The Personal Writings of Joseph Smith* [Deseret Book, 1984], 367).

The Prophet Joseph knew from his own experience what a blessing and privilege it was to have a friend. He said: "Those who have not been enclosed in the walls of prison without cause or provocation, can have but little idea how sweet the voice of a friend is" (*Teachings of the Prophet Joseph Smith* [Deseret Book, 1976], 134).

One of the saddest things about the Prophet's life for me is how many of his closest friends and associates turned against him. I can't imagine how painful it must have been for him to see those who had been by his side through extraordinary experiences let go and turn away. President Wilford Woodruff recorded in his diary (I'm so thankful he kept such good journals!) a statement Joseph Smith had made in May of 1843, where he said that only two of the original Twelve Apostles had not "lifted their heel against" him—namely, Brigham Young and Heber C. Kimball (see *History of the Church,* 5:412).

And yet the Prophet Joseph was so quick to forgive. Remember the story of his friendship with William W. Phelps, who was baptized in 1832 and had many spiritual experiences and opportunities for leadership. He misused some Church funds and was disfellowshipped in March of 1838. He became a bitter enemy to the Prophet, and even testified against Joseph and his fellow prisoners in Liberty Jail. He was finally excommunicated in March of 1839. The Prophet must have been deeply hurt by this former friend who turned against him with such animosity.

By the summer of 1840, Brother Phelps had experienced a mighty change of heart. In June he wrote a letter of true repentance to the Prophet, admitting he had done wrong and expressing how sorry he was. He wrote: "I want your fellowship; if you cannot grant that, grant me your peace and friendship, for we are brethren, and our communion used to be sweet, and whenever the Lord brings us together again, I will make all the satisfaction on every point that saints or God can require."

On July 22, 1840, the Prophet wrote back quite a lengthy letter, including the following:

"Dear Brother Phelps: . . . You may in some measure realize what my feelings, as well as Elder Rigdon's and Brother Hyrum's were, when we read your letter—truly our hearts were melted into tenderness and compassion when we ascertained your resolves. . . . It is true, that we have suffered much in consequence of your behavior. . . .

One with whom we had oft taken sweet counsel together, and enjoyed many refreshing seasons from the Lord— 'had it been an enemy, we could have borne it.' . . . Believing your confession to be real, and your repentance genuine, I shall be happy once again to give you the right hand of fellowship, and rejoice over the returning prodigal. . . . Come on, dear brother, since the war is past, for friends at first, are friends again at last. Yours as ever. Joseph Smith, Jun." (*History of the Church*, 4:141, 163).

About one year later, Brother Phelps was rebaptized. He moved to Utah in 1848. He wrote many hymns, including "The Spirit of God like a Fire Is Burning," "Now Let Us Rejoice," "Redeemer of Israel," and "If You Could Hie to Kolob." One of his hymns, though, has special meaning in light of all that had happened in his life: "Praise to the Man."

Is there anyone who needs to hear from us something like what Joseph said to Brother Phelps: "Come on, dear brother (or dear sister) . . . friends at first are friends again at last." There is something so sweet and beautiful about reconciliation, forgiveness, letting go. Is there anyone you can think of who needs to return to the circle of your friendship and love? Anyone you can forgive?

Mohandas Gandhi is reported to have said: "I hold

myself to be incapable of hating any being on earth. By a long course of prayerful discipline, I have ceased for over forty years to hate anybody." Wouldn't that be a great thing to be able to claim?

I love looking up words in dictionaries. I looked up *friend* and *friendship* and found lots of good stuff. Here's a sampling:

"To be ready, willing, or cheerful, joyous—perhaps to frolick! An in-depth relationship combining trust, support, communication, loyalty, understanding, empathy, and closeness.

"One who has sufficient interest to serve another" (Noah Webster, *American Dictionary of the English Language,* 1828).

A true friend is one with whom you can completely relax. Women especially serve in some ways as each other's therapists. We help each other make sense out of what is happening in our lives. Friends help us live longer and handle stress better. They help us live a more joyful life.

Once I was thinking of examples of great friendships. I came up with a long list—too long to include here—but I'll share a few of them:

- The Savior and Mary, Martha, and Lazarus
- Ruth and Naomi

- John Adams and Thomas Jefferson
- Helen Keller and Annie Sullivan
- Porgy and Bess
- Batman and Robin
- Kermit and Miss Piggy

Okay, I'm getting off track, but maybe you've thought of some great friendships too.

Think of someone who is a friend to you right now. What are some things that make him or her such a good friend? Is it the joy and pleasure of just being friends? Do your friends make you want to live better and be better? Do they both cry and laugh with you? Are you safe with them? Is there trust?

How do we find and keep good friends? Look in your own family. Some have found best friends in their own home! This is true for me in my friendship with my younger sister Charlotte. In spite of some spectacular disagreements when we shared a bedroom and everything else in our growing-up years, we have become the best of friends. I love her so much. She's been very patient as I've written and talked about her through the years.

My friendship with my mother deepened when I went on my first mission. She fasted for me once a week, sent letters and packages, and helped me feel close even though we were 10,000 miles apart.

I treasure my friendship with all my sisters and brothers, aunts and uncles, nieces and nephews, and the little "greats" who are coming along.

There are ways we can be better friends, including living the Golden Rule, keeping confidences (never betraying a trust), and becoming better listeners. We can also work to cultivate a kind and friendly countenance, which reminds me of the story of an Asian girl who was introducing her friend to her bishop. She said in her broken English, "He not mean . . . he just look mean."

It's been my experience that the best way to find a friend is to search, and to be a friend. Open your heart . . . and your doors and your windows.

Friendship isn't simply about gathering people around you who are just like you, is it? There are some wonderful experiences in having friends with different talents, cultures, and traditions. So try not to be too isolated or insulated. And don't lose opportunities for being *with* others by spending too much time in front of the TV or in meaningless reading or computer games or online or whatever. We can all probably do a better job of following what Church leaders have encouraged us to do: Get involved in life, rather than just contemplating it!

We can get involved in service. Jesus taught that by losing ourselves in service to others, we find ourselves (see Matthew 10:39). President Spencer W. Kimball said: "The more we serve our fellowmen in appropriate ways, the more substance there is to our souls. We become more significant individuals. . . . Indeed, it is easier to 'find' ourselves because there is so much more of us to find!" (*Ensign,* July 1978, 3).

Get tickets for plays, concerts, or movies, and invite someone to go along. Join the ward choir, a book club, a neighborhood exercise group. Invite a mom to bring her children and join you at the park. Borrow some children (if you don't have any) and join a play group. See if you can find someone who's lonely whom you could befriend. I think we could write more letters, send more cards, make more phone calls and visits than we do.

Elder Jeffrey R. Holland spoke about friendship: "We could remember that Christ called his disciples friends, and that friends are those who stand by us in times of loneliness or potential despair. We could remember a friend we need to contact or, better yet, a friend we need to make. In doing so we could remember that God often provides his blessings through the compassionate and timely response of another. For someone nearby we may be the means of heaven's answer to a very urgent prayer" (*Ensign,* November 1995, 69).

Friendship is not just about having friends who are your same age or in the same season as you are. Many of us have dear friends who are much older or younger. I remember my sister Susan going to play Scrabble with "Aunt Olive," a friend fifty-seven years older than she was who won every single game they played. Oh, how they loved each other!

Sometimes our paths cross just briefly with others, and yet with such important consequences. Some friends have come into my life literally for twenty minutes but have made such a significant difference. Some people collect coins, stamps, thimbles, frogs, tumbleweeds, boxes . . . I seem to collect friends—wonderful people all over the world. How I wish I had some way to stay close to each of them.

My patriarchal blessing has some strong counsel on being careful in my choice of friends, stating that there are those who would want to convince me that the gospel of Jesus Christ was not the most important thing in my life. Elder Robert D. Hales gave similar advice to all of us: "Do you know how to recognize a true friend? A real friend loves us and protects us. . . . A true friend makes it easier for us to live the gospel by being around him [or her]" (*Ensign,* May 1990, 40).

While I've met a few people who were not "of good report or praiseworthy," I've been blessed with wonderful friends in my life. I could keep you up all night just sharing examples of the amazing, beautiful people who have been part of my life through the years. I could tell you some wonderful stories, and all of them are true. (You might be one of them!)

But it's hard to keep close to *everyone,* isn't it? Oh, how sad I feel at having lost touch with some dear friends as the years have gone by. I so often think of the statement from Anne Morrow Lindbergh: "My life cannot implement in action the demands of all the people to whom my heart responds."

There was a time in my life several years ago when I felt a need for a close friend. (What I *really* wanted was a husband, but that didn't seem to be happening—one of my dreams that hasn't come true yet.) It's not that I haven't always had many wonderful people in my life— good friends—but I think you know what I mean if I say that I needed a close friend, someone I could share my heart with, my deepest feelings, my fears and disappointments, my laughter and my tears, my memories and dreams.

And not right away, but eventually, I received the gift of the friend I had been searching for. Oh, what an incredible blessing! I've never been sure how to thank Heavenly Father adequately for the gift of friendship. It is such a great blessing to have someone with whom I am so completely comfortable, with whom I can be *real*— honest and open and trusting. It is an extraordinary experience to have someone know you so well and love you anyway! I'm safe!

My father taught me a lot about friends through the example of his friendship with his dear pal Lewie. They met in the 1920s when they were roommates in medical school at Northwestern in Chicago. My dad wanted their friendship to be forever—an eternal, unending friendship. And so he kept in touch, and after almost seventy years, Lewie was baptized at age ninety, with my dad, age ninety-two, by his side. I think they are now missionary companions! I think of them whenever I read the Savior's words in 3 Nephi 18:32: "Nevertheless, ye shall not cast him out of your synagogues, or your places of worship, for unto such shall ye continue to minister; for ye know not but what they will return and repent, and come unto me with full purpose of heart, and I shall heal them; and ye shall be the means of bringing salvation unto them."

I think we should never give up on others *or* on ourselves.

From the time we're little, we feel a strong need to *belong*—to know that someone likes us, that someone will "be there" for us—to know that we have a friend. I hope everyone reading this chapter has at least one good, true friend. I hope there is no one who feels friendless. But we've probably all had times in our lives when we've felt that, although we knew a lot of people, we didn't feel especially close to any particular one.

Maybe we've moved to a new place and are just beginning to get acquainted. It might appear that everyone is already "set," with their friendships deep-rooted. It may feel like there's not a place for us. I think we learn compassion, among other things, from these seasons.

When times of loneliness set in, don't ever forget that you have friends in High Places! Remember always how many heavenly friends you have. We are loved so much by our Heavenly Father, the Savior, and the Holy Ghost—not to mention relatives and friends who are Over There! But oh, how close they are to us! Most of them you don't remember right now, but they'll never forget you or turn away from you.

I want to close with Proverbs 17:17: "A friend loveth at all times, and a brother [or sister] is born for adversity." Maybe my Dad was born to help Lewie—to be his friend. Maybe I was born to help you at some moment or season of your life, and maybe you were born to help me. Maybe you were born to be a positive influence on your children and grandchildren, or a neighbor, or a stranger. Or anyone who might be hungry, thirsty, sick, naked, imprisoned . . .

The Savior said: "Ye are my friends, if ye do whatsoever I command you" (John 15:14). And "Verily I say unto you my friends, fear not, let your hearts be comforted; yea, rejoice evermore, and in everything give thanks" (D&C 98:1).

Sweet words. He also said that He will never leave us entirely alone. He has promised, "I will not leave you comfortless: I will come to you" (John 14:18).

I know this is true. I feel it. May God bless each of us to trust in Him and to find joy, contentment, hope, peace, and good friends.

God Bless America

More than forty-five years ago, I was a brand-new missionary, called to serve for two years in the Southern Far East Mission. I thought that was Florida! But no, it was Asia.

It was my first time to really be away from home, and I went halfway around the globe—as far as I could have traveled without starting home again.

I was *homesick*—not just for my family, but for America, for something that was familiar. Everything was different for me—the language, the food, the climate, the communication, the transportation . . . *everything.*

I was in Hong Kong, a place I'd only heard about, with such an exotic name. This is a unique, amazing, hard-to-adequately-describe city. To my inexperienced eyes, every single person looked exactly alike, and to my inexperienced ears, they were shouting strange noises at each other.

The day after I arrived, the mission president's wife took me visiting teaching on a hillside among refugees from mainland China. I'm sure I was wide-eyed and open-mouthed as I went with Sister Taylor on the bus to the harbor, and then on a ferry from the peninsula, Kowloon, to the island of Hong Kong. We went to a place called Aberdeen with a couple of sister missionaries who knew Cantonese.

Oh my, oh my . . . I had never in my whole life even *imagined* that people could live in such conditions. To me this lifestyle appeared much more challenging than camping out forever.

We climbed the hillside on hand-dug dirt stairs. Chickens and children ran out of the way as we trudged to visit a sweet, beautiful young Chinese mother. I saw and felt things I had never felt before as I looked around at these refugee families and realized—*knew*—they were children of God, just as precious and important to Heavenly Father as I or anyone else was. They were my brothers and sisters.

I felt overwhelmed at the distance between me and them—the plains *they* had crossed, and the oceans *I* had crossed, and the distance that still existed between us because I couldn't speak their language and would likely never understand their current situation. And yet we had so much we could teach each other—so much we could share that would make a difference for all of us. I remember that distinct impression as I gave and received many, many smiles that day. It was a breakthrough.

After a few days in Hong Kong and an interview with my mission president, I was assigned to go to Taiwan, formerly known as Formosa. Just as with Cantonese in Hong Kong, I didn't know a single word of Mandarin, so I continued to be isolated from most of what was going on around me.

On my first Sunday we sang "More Holiness Give Me" in sacrament meeting, and I sang with my little English hymnbook, aching to understand at least a little bit of what was happening. When we came to the part about "More longing for home," it pretty much sank me into a hole of homesickness. I thought that if I were even an *ounce* or an *inch* more filled with a longing for home I would positively perish.

Several times during those first few weeks I would roll myself up in some thick curtains in the part of the building that served as our chapel, and I would just cry so hard. I know it's making you emotional just to imagine my agony.

Slowly I began to learn some Mandarin (which is such a beautiful language!), to become accustomed to my surroundings, and to make friends. How helpful!

And I began to learn something that would be one of my most important lessons. I'll illustrate it by telling of an adventure my companion and I had in the city of Tainan in the south of Taiwan. We taught a wonderful young Chinese girl who was baptized, and to celebrate this event, we took her to the American military base for a good American meal. I was so excited. I knew she would *love* everything I loved—that this would be a first-class treat for her.

It didn't quite turn out that way. She'd never eaten with anything but chopsticks. She hated the taste and feel of the mashed potatoes. And on and on.

It was one of my early experiences with the truth that *different* isn't *wrong* . . . it's just different. But I had never realized before that there *was* so much "different" in the world. The experience that day helped me to open my eyes, ears, and heart much wider, and to realize that there were many "right" ways to live, many things that "worked," even though they were initially so foreign to me.

In 1963, when I had been gone from home more

than one year, a group of us missionaries had been invited to visit an aircraft carrier at Subic Naval Base in the Philippines. One of the things I remember most clearly about that visit (besides the fact that we drank all their milk) was seeing the flag—the American flag—waving in the breeze at one end of the extremely long deck. It stirred something deep inside of me and brought emotion to the surface.

One morning in November of 1963, my companion and I got on the bus on our way to our language class. Someone got on with a newspaper that had a *huge* headline: "KENNEDY . . ." but I couldn't see what else it said. My mind raced through things like, "He's going to visit here—the people love him so much because he's a Catholic, and the Philippines is a Catholic country—he's coming—the other word is *visit.*"

But then the bus went by a busy corner and the person shifted enough for me to read the whole headline: "KENNEDY DEAD."

That affected me deeply and significantly. Something terrible had happened in my country and I was thousands of miles away, unable to really share in the national mourning. I don't know that I was particularly frightened, although that may have been part of what I was feeling. I remember Filipinos coming up to us wherever we went, expressing how sorry they felt that our president had been killed. That was so touching. But the main emotion was a sense of loss that I wasn't "home" at a time when something truly awful had happened. When America was hurt, I felt the pain.

One of my favorite places in all the Philippines is the American Cemetery near Manila. (It used to be called Fort McKinley but is now called Fort Bonifacio.) This is the place where Elder Gordon B. Hinckley dedicated the land of the Philippines to the preaching of the gospel in June of 1961. There are thousands of marble crosses lined up in perfect rows surrounding a peaceful, beautiful circle of marble walls bearing the names of those who died in the terrible part of the war that took place in and near the Philippines. It is one of the holiest and most sobering places I've ever been, a reminder of the sacrifices Americans have made in behalf of the citizens of the world.

I had another such reminder years later, when I was back in the Philippines on another mission in 1972–73. Some of the first POWs who were released from Vietnam came to Clark Air Force Base in the Philippines on their way home to America. I couldn't imagine what they had been through. Many LDS families welcomed those men into their homes, and they showed us pictures and told us stories of what it was like to be with them, to greet them at the airport, to have a few hours with them so soon after they had been released from years of isolation and deprivation.

I was moved by the way they described the response of the men to the flags, the singing, and the cheering as they came off the planes. I hadn't been a POW, but just being away from America had helped me to realize more than ever before what my homeland meant to me.

I was in the Philippines in early 1973 when Ferdinand Marcos declared martial law. It was an uncertain time, with new rules and curfews and demands for everyone to turn in their firearms. Even though I was not affected in a major way, I saw and felt enough to treasure the freedom of living in America.

I remember an early morning walk with a dear friend in Central Java, Indonesia, as our branch was heading for a picnic. Tan Khik Liang was Chinese, living in a place where he could not *be* Chinese. He couldn't even speak his native language, Mandarin. I remember he wasn't even supposed to speak it at home.

As we walked together that morning, he asked me

why *he* hadn't been born in America. He had so many hopes and dreams. . . . I found myself wondering if I had ever been grateful enough for the blessing of America.

Another of the incredible adventures of my life, and one of my most important learning experiences, began in September of 1984 when I went to Nigeria, West Africa, to help with a child health project. After a few days in Lagos we traveled to the place we would live, in Cross River State, many miles away. There were so many things to adjust to. We had no electricity and rarely any running water, and even when we got water, it wasn't safe for drinking.

When I think of Africa, I always have memories of my wonderful neighbor Cecilia, whose life was and is so radically different from mine (thinking mainly of living conditions). I used to wonder what Cecilia and others of my African friends might miss if they were plunked in the middle of "Happy Valley, USA." The longer I was there, the less I could picture Cecilia being thrilled and delighted with all our "conveniences." I realized our way of life might well interfere with her profound sense of contentment and peace, her closeness to the good earth, her genuine joy in all that surrounded her.

Would she miss the tropical rainstorms? The singing

frogs? The sound of wind in the bamboo? The spectacular sunsets? The distant drums on a quiet night?

Would she miss the chance to spend time with friends as they washed at the river? The trek to the eight-day market and back? The walk out to their cassava "farm" to see how the plants were doing?

I think there would be much she *would* miss, just as there was much I missed about my home for the months I lived in Africa.

We had a battery-powered radio while we were there. Some nights we'd turn it on for a little while, just to hear the words "Voice of America." It's something else I cannot adequately describe: the feeling that came just from hearing those words. We wouldn't keep the radio on very long at a time, because batteries were very rare and very expensive, but it was fun to hear exotic music, other languages, and some world news.

It was an election year, and I very much wanted to vote. While we were in Lagos, we decided to find the American Embassy to check in and to get absentee ballots. Our taxi driver wasn't sure where it was, but all at once we looked ahead and saw an American flag waving in the breeze. As I wrote in my journal, "It was sort of like, 'There's heaven.'"

I also wrote: "I think you get a sense of patriotism no matter where you would be from. The Canadians would likely feel the same, the Australians, probably even the Nigerians when they see their green-and-white flag. I hope everybody can feel that way, but we did."

As we drew closer to the Embassy, we were surrounded by hundreds of Africans. We found out this was a daily occurrence—throngs of people trying to get close enough to the Embassy to ask about going to America or about getting a job. People were searching for a better life than the one they had, for a chance to go to school, for a place to raise their families. And they had heard wonderful things about America.

It's hard to put into words what it was like to approach the Embassy, this beautiful, neat oasis in a huge, crowded city, and have passports that allowed us to go through the gates to the order, cleanliness, and safety of this little piece of "home." I don't know how else to describe it, but I'll never forget how I felt.

Both my companion, Ann, and I had tried to get absentee ballots before we left home, but they hadn't been printed yet. So now we filled out forms at the Embassy so that the ballots could be sent to our place in Eket, Cross River State.

Well, my ballot came the day after the election, two months later, and Ann's never did arrive. So we did the next best thing: We prayed that two people in America who had not planned to vote would change their minds and would vote in our places (sort of), and that they'd vote for the one we would have voted for, who happened to be Ronald Reagan that year of 1984.

After the election had taken place, we turned on VOA (*Voice of America*) a few times during the night, trying to find out if Reagan had won. At about 2:30 in the morning on Wednesday, November 7, 1984, I learned that he had. Ann was asleep, and I awakened her with, "Ann, Ann, he won!"

Walter Mondale and Geraldine Ferraro were both gracious in defeat and asked that all Americans support President Reagan. And then I heard his voice! Oh! That was so fantastic! He was somewhere in California, and we were somewhere in Africa. He said, "This isn't the end of *anything* . . . it's the beginning of *everything!*"

That really stirred my feelings of love for my country even though I was so very many miles away. (It felt like more than just miles, actually—like I was *worlds* away.) But I was feeling so close to America that morning. I kept thinking I wanted to write a letter to President Reagan.

Part of me would say, "You don't write a letter to the president of the United States," and another part of me would respond, "Well, why not?"

I shared the idea with Ann, and she agreed enthusiastically. She said if I had a feeling that I should write such a letter, then I should. So I did. I sat down at our little portable manual typewriter and wrote my letter. I just put "White House, Washington, D.C." on the envelope. I thought that maybe with the exotic Nigerian stamp and envelope someone would make sure he got it.

I told President Reagan about where we were and why, about our Embassy experience in Lagos, our desire to vote, and what had happened. I told him what it was like to hear his voice in the middle of a dark, dark night. (I think it's darker when there isn't any electricity, and I don't mean that as a "duh!" statement.)

I told him a little bit about the child health project we were working on. I wished him a good experience as president and thanked him for his willingness to serve.

Lo and behold, in January I got a letter back! It reached us through a Mobil Oil station that was across the road from our place there in Eket. One morning an official car arrived from Mobil, and some people got out and said, "Which one is Mary Ellen Edmunds?" I said, "I am." I didn't know what this was about yet, but I was certainly curious. They said, "This is a letter that came to you through Mobil."

I thanked them and took the letter. It was from the White House. It was a very nice personal letter from President Reagan! And enclosed was a check drawn on his personal account, made out to our project and signed in his handwriting. He had sent us a donation of $100. What a feeling that gave to us, thousands of miles from home, that the president of our country had sent us some money for the work we were doing in Africa. Woweee! Unforgettable.

I have been enriched in countless ways by my experience living with the Chinese people in Taiwan and Hong Kong, the people of the Philippines on two missions, and the people of Indonesia and Africa. Although I love the various cultures, my heart is always drawn to my own country, to America.

In 1991, I was able to fulfill one of my lifelong desires: to see the Statue of Liberty. I could feel the emotion inside of me as my friend Carol and I got off the boat and approached the statue. Inside a visitors' center there was an area where I could hear voices as if they were people who had arrived and seen this statue and all that it represented. People had indeed recorded excerpts from letters and journals, and that was what I could hear.

It hit me so deeply that I "lost it." I started to cry and then to sob, and we went outside and sat at a little table for a while until I could calm down.

I think there are several reasons why I was affected so strongly. For one thing, I began thinking of my ancestors who had come past that statue and to Ellis Island. Both my grandmothers were born in Switzerland and came at different times, and I wondered what their feelings had been. One of my grandfathers was born in Wales and came to America searching for a better life. And even my own father, on his return from a mission in Germany and Switzerland, came through Ellis Island before entering the country again.

All I know is that I felt part of *me* returning from Asia, from Africa, and from other places I had been. This was *my home,* my country, my native land.

I feel like the message of Joshua 24:13 applies to me, and I've tried to be thankful for this blessing: "I have given you a land for which ye did not labour, and cities which ye built not, and ye dwell in them; of the vineyards and oliveyards which ye planted not do ye eat."

I'm so grateful and happy to be a citizen of the

United States of America. To me, patriotism is more than flag-waving and fireworks. It's being a good citizen, doing the best I can to enjoy and protect freedom, to obey the laws of the land, to elect and support wise and honest leaders, to understand and defend the Constitution, to honor my heritage, and to be involved in service. It's gratitude.

I love my country. I love America's traditions and values. So many paid such a high price for what I enjoy.

President Hugh B. Brown, who was born in America but spent much of his life in Canada, shared the following feelings about America: "To those who are losing faith in America, to those who criticize her, we issue this challenge: Cast your eyes to the four corners of the earth. Can you see anything to compare with her? Where do you find greater evidence of freedom? In what land do the inhabitants have greater voice in governing themselves? Where do you see a way of life which has produced a greater abundance for its people? In which country do you find greater numbers of children receiving an excellence of education to surpass that which is to be found here? Where is there less want, less misery? Where in all the world do you find men who are given comparable rights to enjoy their freedom to worship as that freedom finds expression in the land of America? Can you really doubt that this land is in very deed a land of promise?" (*The Abundant Life* [Salt Lake City: Bookcraft, 1965], 50).

About ten years ago I was on a cruise with my mother and some other family members. Because our cabin had been changed, my mother and I were sitting in an area near a bank of elevators waiting to identify our bags and have them taken to the right cabin.

We were watching some young men who were working *very* hard, unloading stacks of luggage from the elevators. I told my mother that I thought these workers were probably from the Philippines. But I was curious enough to eventually ask them, "Where are you from?"

"We are from Indonesia, ma'am."

I loved them instantly! I can still remember their absolute surprise when I began to speak to them in their own language. An American woman on a cruise ship speaking Bahasa Indonesia!

I'd learned some songs while I served there, and I sang them for these boys. I think I ended up making them homesick, because they were songs about the love of mothers for their children.

By now our luggage had been found, and we were

ready to leave. But I had a strong impression to do one more thing. I thanked these boys for their help, and then I told them I had a surprise for them. I sang their national anthem to them. I had learned it because I felt it would help me love that land and the people. I was right. And I became emotional as I sang "Indonesia, tanah air ku, tanah tumpah darah ku. . . ." They became emotional too, and stood quietly as I sang.

I have a great love for Indonesia, the Philippines, Nigeria, and other places I have lived and visited. I'm thankful for the wonderful people who have deepened my sense of brotherhood and sisterhood—of the fact that we are all children of the same God, and that He loves each of us and all of us perfectly and wonderfully. We are connected in so many ways.

And yet, without taking anything away from anyone who lives anywhere else in this wide, wonderful world, I sing with all my heart: "God bless America, land that I love."

Porches

If we were together, I'd ask you to sing with me. When I tell you the words at the beginning of the song, I think you might catch on to the tune:

"Where have all the porches gone?" And so on.

For years I've had this thing on my mind about porches. When I walk in the mornings, I notice them. I also notice their absence. This is one of the things that seems to have changed with the speed and pace of our lives.

When I was little, it seemed that more homes had porches, and more people used them. I loved it when Palmers would be out on the porch, maybe with Roland playing his guitar and singing "Hallelujah, I'm a bum." (I'm not kidding!)

I loved it that Joneses were out on their porch as I'd roller-skate by (although I didn't appreciate having them laugh when I'd crash).

Porches

I love Kent and Karen's porch in Draper with the big, comfortable swinging bench. There's a friendly tree near for shade.

Sometimes my neighbor Fran would sit out on her small porch in the evening, and pretty soon others would gather.

Other neighbors would line up chairs along the front of their homes, almost like a porch extension, with a friendly, welcoming feeling. Anyone was welcome to stop by and sit and visit for a while.

I think we'd all be better off if there were more porches, and if we used them. We'd be more in touch with each other. Porches bring people together.

Do you have a porch? Or could you just put some chairs out in the front yard? A porch doesn't need to be fancy. In fact, it seems that some of the porches on brand-new homes might be there only for decoration—some look like they've never been used. I think some aren't even wide enough for a chair.

I've got a little porch (room for two if the chairs are close together and you don't need to open the front door). I think I'm suffering from porchlessness. Do you feel that way ever? Maybe you live in an apartment on the fifteenth floor, and it might be dangerous to try to put chairs out there on that little balcony thing. But where it's possible, could you create a porchlike feeling? Maybe someone could play a guitar or harmonica once in a while. Maybe you'd even like to sing.

I love doing that with friends and family—gathering and singing the familiar songs and visiting. Even without a campfire. Solving world problems. Sharing burdens and joys. Sitting quietly. Just being together.

I once heard a family described as "world-class porch sitters." I love the sound and feel of that. If you live in a neighborhood where there are several porches, you could form a porch association. Nothing formal with dues and rules, just a fun way to encourage each other and act organized.

Ask me about my porch experiences the next time you see me. I've had some wonderful ones. And consider doing something that will create a porchlike feeling where you live.

On Being Single

When I was a young girl I used to listen to radio programs. We didn't have television yet, and mostly I'd play outside, but I did love listening to shows like *Johnny Dollar, Gunsmoke,* and *Suspense* on our big radio in the living room.

One show was about a woman named Helen Trent who was thirty-five and single. In the introduction to the show they made a Big Deal about the fact that she was thirty-five and single. Back then I thought how horrible that would be—to be single at such an *old* age!

Now I think, "Oh, to be thirty-five again!"

As you might imagine, I've been invited to speak at quite a few conferences for single members of the Church. I'm never sure quite how to start such a talk. Sometimes I feel like I'm in a self-help program, and I should begin with, "Hi. My name is Mary Ellen Edmunds, and I'm single."

On Being Single

Oh no! Not *single!?* Yes, single.

Pop quiz: What movie did this phrase come from: "Sad to be all alone in the world"? (Answer: *Thoroughly Modern Millie.* Remember?)

It *would* be sad to be all alone in the world, but no one needs to be alone. One thing I feel deeply about is that *single* doesn't need to mean *alone.* No one needs to choose to be isolated or insulated from others. I love the song with the phrase "no man is an island." No woman is either.

I realize, though, that there are so many who suffer from loneliness—so many who *do* feel "all alone in the world." That's a terrible hunger. Some of those who feel alone and lonely are single . . . and some are not.

The word *single* is not a synonym for "alone," "lonely," "worthless," or "incomplete." Dictionary definitions do include such words: "one only," "individual," "without another or others," "alone," "solitary." Interestingly, though, other definitions include terms like "honest" and "sincere."

We sometimes define or describe *single* as "ugly," "unwanted," "unable to have a meaningful day or week or life," "unloved," "unappreciated," "second best or lower," "unable to fully serve or achieve," "awkward," or "ignored by others." But none of those need be true in our lives.

Sometimes I've thought of the things people have accomplished when they've been "all alone" (and yet not really completely alone), such as when Joseph Smith went into a grove to pray, and the Savior into a garden to begin the most significant sacrifice in history.

Some of our most productive, happy, and spiritual times can be when we're alone. Many spiritual events, manifestations, visits, and such didn't happen to people when they were in a crowd or group, but when they were alone. I imagine each of us can think of some significant things that have happened to us when we've been by ourselves, pleading in prayer, giving thanks, or pondering.

I've had people say to me that there are things I could never have done if I'd been married and raising children. I know that's true. I likely would not have gone on more than one mission. I probably wouldn't have had the blessing of going to Africa or working at the Missionary Training Center for so many years. There are other opportunities that may not have come my way.

And there are times when someone will ask if I would trade it all for a family. I'm not sure how I respond out loud, but in my heart I feel certain that there's not a need to "trade." I don't have to. My efforts in every call that has come my way "count," and the joy and the lessons are mine to keep and cherish.

I do realize that there are things I cannot learn if I spend all my time alone. Being with others, learning and experiencing together, is important. I may become too comfortable thinking only of myself—or thinking mainly of myself and organizing and arranging things so that I put all of my own wants and needs first. Zion is a society, not just a group of individuals.

No matter what your circumstances are, you probably have dreams that have not come true. My personal dream—and I'm almost positive my Primary teacher told me this would happen if I did my best to keep all the commandments—was to be married with ten children, live in a small town, and volunteer at the library.

I shared that dream a couple of times in talks, and wouldn't you know it—each time there was some woman who came up and said, "I'm living your dream!" Yep . . . ten children, living in a small town, and volunteering at the library. Imagine! My dream came true in someone else's life!

When dreams don't come true, when life doesn't turn out as we had hoped and planned, what are we supposed to do? Shriveling is one option. (I chose that word because I wanted to see if I could spell it without help. Also, I like the way it sounds when I say it.)

For me, shriveling is not an option. Hey, I look bad enough without being shriveled.

But I have to say that I've observed many who have chosen to shrivel. What I mean is that something creeps into their days, their souls, and even their countenances, something that diminishes their quality of life, their attractiveness. I've become aware of a lot of self-pity in some, creating an increasingly limited choice of conversational topics. "Let me tell you how bad I feel today; you haven't heard since yesterday."

I've even known some who have acted like they hate everyone who *is* married, who *does* have children. Oh my goodness!

Some seem to retreat from associating with almost anyone. Bitterness may set in, many times accompanied by a disappointment and even an anger toward God. Ouch!

I'll admit I've had shrivel moments in my life. "Poor MEE! Poor MEE!" I speak and write things in a light-hearted way, but I've had times of deep sorrow, of pain and tears, of hopelessness. I have days when I'm down and feeling sad, exhausted, and discouraged . . . I'm normal! I've just worked hard not to let such feelings last—not to let them get in the way of pressing forward.

And I've worked to have friends in all kinds of circumstances, not just single friends. It's enriching and enjoyable to associate with a rich variety of people, don't you think?

There have been adjustments related to being single and living alone. Sometimes I wonder, "Do you mean to tell me that I'm going to have to do all these things for myself?" There's so much I don't know, and it has never been easy for me to ask for help from others. Thank goodness for my parents, for sisters and brothers, for good neighbors and wonderful friends. It's really hard to be in charge of *everything!*

I'm sure you'd recognize some of the situations I've faced, like having others get awkward all of a sudden when they've found out I'm not married. The question that leads to this realization is usually something like "What was your maiden name?" or "How many children do you have?" or "What does your husband do?"

I admit I have some fun occasionally responding to "husband" questions. Usually I just give a standard answer like, "I'm not married," or "I'm single," but you have to know that there are times when the temptation is too great. . . . Like when someone asks, "What does your husband do?" I love to respond with, "I have no idea!" Or if they ask, "Is your husband here?" I can say, "Well, wouldn't that be a surprise!"

I've had funny and tender things happen with nieces and nephews. I remember that when Wendy used to come over to play, she always seemed to bring her "Old Maid" cards. Was there a message in that? Ha! Naughty little girl!

Once when three of my nephews came to visit, little Kevin, who was then six, was kind of following Richard and Michael around, but he looked like he was thinking deeply and looking for someone or something. Finally he looked up at me with all innocence and asked, "Where's your father?" I explained that my father was Grandpa Eds, and that he lived with Grandma Eds. "No, I mean your father that lives here." He wondered where my *husband* was.

Precious little guy. I explained that I didn't have one. He couldn't figure that out. On another visit about a year later he asked me, "Are you lonely living here alone?" I said, "Not when you're here."

One time I made myself laugh by pretending there

had been a major announcement by Church leaders. The fictitious announcement went something like this:

Did you hear the announcement about single members of the Church? Oh, this is so exciting! After many hours and years of work, clearance has been given for single Church members to pray! Yes! And they can go to the temple! Oh my goodness! Single members have been given permission to partake of the sacrament, serve others, be home and visiting teachers and even [gasp] Gospel Doctrine teachers! Single members can now work on their food storage, sing the hymns, read the scriptures . . .

You can tell I got carried away with this (I'm including just a shortened version). You could tell I'd get carried away before you ever started reading this part, couldn't you? Admit it.

That little list reminds me of all the reasons I have to be happy and grateful—to be involved in doing good and being good. I'll admit that one of my most effective tools for being happy and enjoying life is a sense of humor. I'm so grateful to my Heavenly Father for a cheerful nature. I've worked to develop and keep it!

One day I was just leaving the temple, having had a wonderful time, when a woman approached me with a certain, sort of puzzled, look on her face. She asked, "Are you Sister Edmunds?" I smiled and said I was "one of them." We chatted briefly, and then she said, "You seem so happy all the time." I responded that I do tend to be a happy person.

She hesitated, but then her real source of wondering appeared. "But you're single." I'm not kidding! That's what she said! "Yes, I am," I replied, "but I'm also happy." Have you ever had an experience like that?

Sometimes the way people respond to my singleness, especially in their body language and tone of voice, indicates their belief that I'm to be pitied, for surely I'm missing all the things that bring true happiness in this life. And there are lots of times when others seem to think I'm only pretending to be happy—that you can't really be happy, as a woman, without being married.

One woman stopped me and asked what she could tell her thirty-something daughter (was she Helen Trent's mother?) to help her "feel better" about not being married. I don't remember exactly what I said (or what I have said to others who had similar questions), but I know it had something to do with trust. I trust that Heavenly Father loves me, that He loves each of us and all of us.

Proverbs 3:5–6 teaches us to "Trust in the Lord with all thine heart; and lean not unto thine own understanding.

In all thy ways acknowledge him, and he shall direct thy paths." I'm convinced this applies to *all* of God's children—that a love for Him and a trust in Him will bring us to a point where we follow His guidance, and where we *do* experience great joy and peace in our lives.

I'd like to say that I know happy people in *many* circumstances—married, single, poor, rich, tall, short, sick, healthy, with and without children, employed and unemployed and underemployed. And I've also met unhappy people in all kinds of situations. It's my feeling that a happy spirit doesn't seem to need certain circumstances in order to thrive.

I love what Elder Neal A. Maxwell said about agency: "At the center of our agency is the freedom to form a healthy attitude toward whatever circumstances we are placed in!" (*Ensign,* November 1976, 14).

That's profound. We can *choose* our response to any circumstance, any situation. It may be more difficult to choose happiness in some seasons and circumstances, but it's still possible.

Admittedly, though, some things are easier to have a good attitude about than others. One of the challenging aspects of being single for me has been the "blind date" experience. Have you found that almost everyone you know has someone they'd like you to meet? Okay, maybe not everyone, but quite a few!

I'm sure I'm not the only single person who's ever had some nightmare dates where I was "lined up" by someone so certain they had found the perfect match for me. We could have quite a lively conversation about that, couldn't we?

Don't you just love it (meaning don't you just cringe) when someone tells you you'd be perfect for their grandfather who is seventeen years older than you are and wants to get married so he can go on a lot of missions and then have someone to take care of him during his "last days"? (I had several people say to me, when I was younger, that I'd be such a "good catch" because I was a nurse.)

I have never responded well to the feeling that sometimes comes: "So this is what it has come to: leftovers." I'm sure many have felt that way about *me!*

How about those who say sweet things like, "I just know you're being saved for one of the stripling warriors!" Oh, really? Or, "I just know there's a special man being saved for you." Saved *for* me or *from* me? And why does he always have to be "special"?

I'll let go of my sarcastic comments now—I just had

to include a few, because there are those moments when only humor can pull me out of a difficult mood.

There have been times when I've wondered if anything I've done matters since I'm not married and I'm not raising my own children. I am aware, though, of couples who have not been able to have children, and I suspect my aching is no deeper than theirs. Mine may not even compare to theirs.

Then I think of the heartache of parents who have lost children, either physically or spiritually. And I'm reminded that we *all* struggle to find and hold on to a perfect brightness of hope, no matter what our circumstances might be.

It is simply not true that marriage and children automatically bring happiness anymore than it is true that those who are single or without children have no worth and no purpose, that none of their accomplishments "count."

Just another thought about this. I've had single people say to me things like, "I didn't *choose* to be single!" Perhaps not. Perhaps some don't feel they'd have chosen to live in abject poverty, walking miles for their water and fixing every bite of food from scratch. Some may say they would not have chosen to be widowed so young . . . or at any age. Or to be a single parent. Some may have felt they'd not have chosen to spend life without sight or hearing. My cousin Ida wondered if she chose to die of cancer when she was only thirty-eight, leaving six children behind.

From my experience, I feel that there is sweet compensation for each of us based on what our situations have been—our circumstances, resources, opportunities, and so on. I don't need to spend a lot of time discussing this, but I just want to point out that there is no "labeled group" in this world with a corner on loneliness or struggling.

And speaking of labels, I sometimes get weary of being labeled "single." Can't I just be MEE? Can't I just be a neighbor, a friend, a fellowcitizen? The old lady with the red nose? But I guess it sounds now like I'm searching for a label *other* than single, so I'll not spend any more time on this label stuff.

It is important at any moment in our life to know that what we are doing pleases our Father in Heaven— that we are involved in activities that help Him accomplish His work. My efforts or accomplishments will not include having children, at least not while I'm an "earthling." But my patriarchal blessing gives assurance that someday I'll have such an opportunity. Meanwhile, I enjoy the privilege of helping with other people's children. I love the chance to lift and nurture, to snuggle and enjoy, to love and be loved. Oh, I do, I do!

No condition—not the fact that I'm not married, not the truth that I've never given birth to a child, not the reality that I've made mistakes, not even the times when I've complained and murmured—nothing has ever stopped my Heavenly Father from loving me and caring about me. And the same is true, I'm convinced, for every single one of His children.

The reality is that He *is* my Father, and He knows me and cares deeply about what's happening *in* me as well as *around* me and *to* me. My *worthiness* may change based on choices I make, but nothing affects my *worth* to Him as one of His children.

We are born with worth. It's part of our heritage, part of the blessing we have as children of God. We are worth more than we can imagine in His sight and in His plan.

I am convinced that no good thing will ever be withheld from any of us if we are striving to be faithful and obedient, if we are consciously doing what we can to help build the kingdom, establish Zion, and prepare for the return of Jesus Christ.

I trust my Heavenly Father and the Savior. The core of my peace of soul, my joy and contentment, is a complete trust in Them. They don't "jerk me around," and They don't ask me to do stupid things. They've allowed me to participate in some priceless experiences, some beautiful miracles. How can I *not* be happy? They love me! They like me! They care about me a lot!

May we qualify for gifts of love, peace, joy, hope, and contentment, no matter what our situation. May we seek for the faith, the gratitude, and the perspective to do well in every condition in which we might be found. Let us not let a particular circumstance dictate our sense of worth, our happiness, our delight in doing good, or our knowledge of the love and approbation of our Heavenly Father, who loves us so dearly. Life is wonderful! This is a great plan of happiness, of *happification!*

JOY to the world!

The Second Mile

ave you ever been aware of having a second chance to go the second mile—to be nice, to respond to an opportunity to help someone?

In April of 2002 I was flying from Sacramento to Salt Lake City. I was in seat 11A, and there was a man in 11C, but 11B was empty. I figured it would fill up, though, because the people just kept coming.

And then she came, almost at the last minute. She looked a bit frustrated and even confused. She had her arms full, and she sat down on top of her seat belt and her complimentary headset. She looked Latin to me, and I felt compassion for her. I wanted to help.

I smiled and asked if I could help her with her seat belt. Then I realized that she probably didn't speak any English. She just smiled shyly and kind of shrugged. So I pointed to my own seat belt, and then she said "Si," and I helped her find hers and get it buckled.

I decided not to try to deal with the complimentary headset. I offered her mine instead, but neither of us used it.

I helped her get her things situated on the floor, and from time to time I tried saying a word or two of Spanish, including "lo siento" ("I'm sorry"), trying to apologize for not being able to talk to her.

She was so sweet—and patient. I was trying to be aware of not smothering her with my concern, if you know what I mean. I didn't want to seem like some superior know-it-all, but I also didn't want to ignore her.

When the plane landed, I made sure she had her things and then walked near her as we left the plane.

And here's where I made a mistake. Looking back on the situation, I wish I had stopped and tried to find out exactly where she needed to be next. I was torn, partly because I didn't know how to ask or wouldn't have understood her answer.

What I chose to do was to walk slowly toward the terminal and baggage claim. I was at the "C" concourse, so normally I'd have kept going straight and down the escalator. But I had some cards to mail, so I turned right toward "D" until I got to the mailbox. I took off my backpack, got out the cards, and put them in.

And then I turned and saw that she was right behind me.

I don't know how to describe the feeling I had when I realized she had followed me. She didn't know where to go, and so she was right behind me. I smiled and hugged her, and she said something I recognized—the word for luggage. I nodded enthusiastically, so thankful I could continue helping her. A second chance!

Here was something rather strange and wonderful: I was allowed to go a second mile when I hadn't gone the whole first mile. Let's take some more time to think about that one of these days. But right now, back to our story.

I asked about "familia," and she said (I think) "un hija." I think that meant she had a daughter.

"Here? Aqui?"

"Si!"

And off we went for the escalator down to baggage claim.

This time I was committed to stay with her until I could be sure she was safe and sound. I did any and every single thing I could think of to assure her of that fact. I hope it doesn't sound too dramatic, but at that moment I would have done anything I could for her. Anything.

We got to the bottom of the escalator, and I was looking to see which carousel had the baggage from our flight.

At about the same moment, I saw and heard a beautiful young woman come racing toward this sweet new friend of mine. The daughter had found the mother! It was an incredible feeling to witness this joyous reunion.

I stayed long enough to ask where she was from (Mexico), and to receive her hugs and "gracias" over and over. I knew "de nada," but I knew a lot more from that moment on. I knew that for at least part of that experience I had done what Jesus wanted me to do. I was inexpressibly happy. Over the top. Off the charts.

I think I can now say that sometimes when we don't quite go the first mile, we're allowed to go the second mile. Thank goodness. And sometimes if we can't quite go the extra mile, maybe we can go the extra inch or anything else that's possible.

Watch for a chance to go the second mile. Be conscious of the first one, too. Remember Who said, "And whosoever shall compel thee to go a mile, go with him twain" (Matthew 5:41).

"Go with him twain." Go willingly and cheerfully. What joy and freedom there is in that second mile!

The Deadly Sin of Pride

I seem to ponder a lot on the things that worry me the most. Pride is one of them. It keeps popping up in my mind, my heart, my actions, my life. Agh!

I consider pride to be one of the Big Ones—a parent and promoter of lots of other challenging sins or weaknesses. Pride is arrogant, boastful, and selfish. It leads to a miserable way of living.

It's been a soul-search for me for a long time, and in my studying I've decided there are three main realities about pride that I need to focus on. (1) Pride separates us from God. (2) Pride separates us from each other. (3) Pride actually separates us from who we really are—from our own Godlike nature. "None is acceptable before God, save the meek and lowly in heart" (Moroni 7:44).

I'm going to share with you one of my personal struggles with pride.

It was 1976, and life was good. I was thirty-six years

old, I'd been home from my most recent mission for about two and a half years, I had decided to return to the profession of nursing, and I felt good!

And then, WHAM! I was called to go on another mission—this time to Indonesia. They had called a nurse from England who was a convert, and they felt it would help to have someone "seasoned" to go with her. "Seasoned" meant *old*. That would be MEE.

We would be the first sister missionaries called to Indonesia. "No thanks," thought I. "Been there, done that. Three missions is plenty. Enough and to spare. But thanks for asking . . ."

Then I made a tiny little huge mistake: I went to the temple to pray about it. Don't ever do that if you're not ready to hear the answer. My answer came: "Yes, We want you to do this."

So then I started thinking, "Hey! This is my *reward* for the tough missions I've already served!" I approached the Language Training Mission with big plans. I had served other missions; I had worked at learning other languages; I'd been teaching at the LTM and knew my way around; this was going to be smooth sailing.

I entered the LTM in September of 1976 with all humility: "I'll show these younger missionaries a thing or two!" There were two of us (yes, just two) in the entire LTM learning Bahasa Indonesia. My companion *was* from England, but she had grown up in Malaysia. The Indonesian language is almost exactly the same as the language of Malaysia. They're even closer than Spanish and Portuguese—more like Spanish in Mexico compared with Spanish in Argentina or something like that.

At this point I need to share a scripture with you. Some of you are getting ahead of me and have already guessed what the scripture is. Stop it! Let me tell my story!

Proverbs 16:18: "Pride goeth before . . . a fall."

It was quickly apparent who was the *slow one* in our class of two. I'll give you a hint: her initials are MEE. I still remember our first test. I got two things right: My name and the date.

Well, the entire eighteen months went sort of like that. That mission was *hard,* with the language, but also physically difficult because of the hot, humid climate.

It was extremely challenging and humbling. And it's one of the best things I've ever done. I'm so thankful for what I learned and felt, and for those I came to love so dearly.

Early on, our mission president assigned two local

companions to work with us, Darsi and Endang. One of the responsibilities he gave me was to teach them English. He said it would help them all the rest of their lives. (And, indeed, they both were able to get excellent employment later, partly because of their English skills.)

Darsi was exceedingly shy. She was tiny and quiet and frightened to be in front of others. But she began to learn English very rapidly. Within a short while she was reading Church books along with the scriptures and Church magazines.

Both Darsi and Endang helped me with Indonesian as well, and as time went along, my language improved, and I became more confident and comfortable in using it.

Toward the end of my mission, I received a letter from a dear friend, Arlene Flanders. She was a member of the Relief Society general board, and she and her husband, Dean, were coming on a journey to Asia, and they wanted to visit me!

She said she would love to speak to the Relief Society sisters and asked if I'd be willing to interpret for her. Would I! Of course! Oh, that would be such an incredible way to finish my mission!

Early in 1978, shortly before I was to be released,

they came—all the way to Solo, in Central Java. The time came for Sister Flanders to speak to the women, and they were gathering with such excitement. It was rare to have such a visitor come beyond Jakarta.

And then an interesting thing happened.

I suppose, as I look back, that the Spirit had been trying to contact me for quite a while, but my pride in what I was about to do had kept me from hearing.

So the Spirit SHOUTED. "Edmunds! Who should be doing what you're doing?" This was a question I had formulated earlier to help myself not take over and "show off" instead of "showing how." Obviously it hadn't worked well in every situation.

Instantly I knew the answer, even though I had a nanosecond more of pride and a little tantrum. ("But I want to do this! I've been looking forward to it! This is my last hurrah!")

But I *knew* that Darsi was the one who should translate for Sister Flanders. I knew it was right.

I whispered to Sister Flanders, and she understood immediately. However, it took some talking and some heavenly help before Darsi agreed. By then I was almost frantic because I knew it *had* to be her, not MEE. I said something silly like, "I'll be right behind you, and I'll help you if you need me." HA.

I say *HA* because there is no way I could have done what she did. She translated into Indonesian, but when she sensed that some couldn't understand, she switched to their native language: Javanese!

Many of the sisters came up to Darsi after the meeting and thanked her sincerely for helping them to have such a wonderful experience. And Darsi wrote me a letter thanking me for giving her the opportunity to help Sister Flanders. She had done something she didn't know she could do, and it was heaven giving her the experience. If not for strong promptings from the Spirit, I would have taken that experience away from her. I shudder to think of it.

Even now, I think of the difference in what it would have meant to me compared to what it meant for her. For me it would have been a sweet journal entry. Looking back years later I might have thought, "Oh, yes, that was a sweet experience."

But for Darsi, it was an amazing and life-changing experience. A few weeks after I had returned home from Indonesia, I heard that Darsi had combined a couple of doctrinal talks about welfare services that President

Marion G. Romney had given, and she had spoken in a district conference. That is *incredible!*

I could keep you here for the rest of the day and the rest of the month with true stories of my personal struggles with the sin of pride. Do you ever struggle too?

Does it sometimes seem like pride is the most annoying interruption in your life, jumping in when you think you're doing fine, trying to smother your little store of meekness and humility? Pride tends to lure or just plain yank us off the straight and narrow way. Can't you just feel it some days—feel pride trying to pry your fingers off the iron rod?

President Howard W. Hunter taught this so well: "Surely the lessons of history ought to teach us that pride, haughtiness, self-adulation, conceit, and vanity contain all of the seeds of self-destruction for individuals, cities, or nations. . . . The only true test of greatness, blessedness, [and] joyfulness is how close a life can come to being like the Master, Jesus Christ" (*Ensign,* November 1990, 18).

Pride is one of the historic Seven Deadly Sins, and it *is* exceedingly deadly.

In President Ezra Taft Benson's incredible sermon on pride from general conference in April 1989 comes the following: "Most of us think of pride as self-centeredness, conceit, boastfulness, arrogance, or haughtiness. All of these are elements of the sin, but the heart, or core, is still missing. The central feature of pride is enmity—enmity toward God and enmity toward our fellowmen. *Enmity* means 'hatred toward, hostility to, or a state of opposition.' It is the power by which Satan wishes to reign over us. . . . The proud wish God would agree with them. They aren't interested in changing their opinions to agree with God's" (*Ensign,* May 1989, 4–7). I strongly recommend a rereading and a careful study of President Benson's message.

Elder Dallin H. Oaks also describes how pride can separate us from God and from each other: "The pride of self-satisfaction is the opposite of humility. This attitude insulates us from learning and separates us from God." Further, "A person who has the pride of self-satisfaction cannot repent, because he recognizes no shortcomings. He cannot be taught, because he recognizes no master. He cannot be helped, because he recognizes no resource greater than his own. . . . Preoccupied with self, the pride of self-satisfaction is always accompanied by an aloofness and a withdrawal from concern for others" (*Pure in Heart* [Bookcraft, 1988], 109, 91–92).

Elder Joseph B. Wirthlin cautioned: "Pride and vanity, the opposites of humility, can destroy our spiritual health as surely as a debilitating disease can destroy our physical health" (*Ensign,* November 1990, 66).

Oh, isn't that the truth? Think of the shock when you've heard that a friend had cancer or some other terrible disease. But did you hear that Edmunds has pride, and is critically ill spiritually? That's even worse!

One of the strongest impressions that has come to me in my thinking might surprise you. It is that one of the worst and most damaging things about pride is that it can keep us from receiving joyfully and gracefully any commendation or praise from heaven—from our Heavenly Father, from the Savior, from the Holy Ghost.

This is one of the worse consequences of allowing pride to separate us from God. There are times when He wants to say to us, "Good for you! Good job! Well done! Thank you!"

And what do we do? We talk back! "Oh, You're just saying that. It wasn't that great. You and I both know it could and should have been better. I'm such a mess! If only . . ."

Don't talk back! Sometimes we may think it's a way

to show humility and meekness, but it just might be pride!

What if the Savior had behaved that way during the days of creation? Suppose He returns after a busy day separating light from darkness, or water from dry ground, and His Father says to Him, "Well done." And instead of smiling and feeling happy, He has to talk back. "Do You think the dark is a bit too dark?" "Did we make too many stars?" "Do You think anyone will mind that the water's wet?"

That did *not* happen, did it? His Father said "well done," and They likely rejoiced together over how wonderful it all was at the end of every single period of creation.

Too often we neither give nor receive enough positive comments from each other, and too often it's pride that keeps these good things from happening!

"Thank you for that beautiful musical number." "The one who usually accompanies me was sick, but I guess it turned out okay."

"Thanks for the lesson." "I ran out of time, as usual. Why does Nora always have to interrupt me!"

From President Ezra Taft Benson again: "God will have a humble people. Either we can choose to be humble or we can be compelled to be humble" (*Ensign,* May 1989, 7).

Wow. We can either *choose* to be humble—to allow our life's experiences to deepen our faith, our courage, our hope, our meekness, and our charity—or we can choose to resist change and live consumed by our pride until a day shall come when we are *compelled* to be humble. OUCH!

Moroni, at the end of the Book of Mormon, asks us to "deny [ourselves] of all ungodliness" (Moroni 10:32). Pride is ungodly. Godliness is humility—being teachable, forgiving, submissive, kind, peacemakers, one heart and one mind with our fellow travelers.

Can we do that? Can we get a little better every day? Can we help each other to become increasingly meek and humble? More pure in heart. More faithful and true. Holier. Happier.

Jesus is the Christ, the Son of the Living God, our Advocate with the Father, and He has done all He can to help us return to our Heavenly Home. May we *respond!*

The Blues

One of the first songs I learned when I was picking out chords on a guitar had the words, "I never felt more like singing the blues." Why *blue?* Because blue is my favorite color, I used to wonder who chose "blue" to describe a feeling of melancholy, of being down, of sadness and "depression lite." (I call it *lite* because I never want to minimize the reality and challenge of serious depression.)

A friend told me she was in the Tabernacle in Salt Lake City when Helen Keller came to speak. (I would have *loved* to be there, but I think I was too young to know anything about it.) I've heard recordings of Helen's voice, and it's incredible that she could speak at all, let alone well enough to be understood.

Apparently she opened up some time for questions. Someone asked her if she could feel colors. With wonderful humor, she responded, "Sometimes I feel blue." Oh, that's so great!

Sometimes I feel blue too. I can't always put a finger on why, but there are times when I'm just "down." For me it often happens in the evening. Some feel blue during winter, partly because there aren't as many flowers as in other seasons, but probably mostly because there isn't as much light. I would think if that happens to you, you wouldn't want to live in the north part of Finland or somewhere like that. Some people have to get special lights to lift their spirits. That's interesting to me, because I think light *does* inspire and lift us.

In my experience, changes in mood are common and natural. I'm not talking about drastic "swings," but just the ups and downs that are part of life. I don't know of anyone who can avoid them. I do meet people who try to hide them, though, and they don't always do it very successfully. I've often spotted a fake smile from a block away, or detected a forced laugh almost instantly.

As human beings, we naturally react to our individual world, its daily changes, and the continual need for different responses. All of us—every single one of us—will come up against circumstances or situations that make us feel low, that put us in a "blue" mood. We might feel uncomfortable, bored, or negative, yet when we discuss our situation, the term we use most often is *depressed.*

There's a difference between having the "blues" and being depressed. When you're down because of something that's happened (or something that hasn't happened), that's the blues. It's a report of how you feel at a particular moment. It generally does not affect most of your daily responsibilities. And luckily, the blues don't hang around for long; they're likely to last for a couple of hours, or maybe a few days throughout the month. It's not a constant state of being. It's a mood that's very responsive to the environment or the weather or outside circumstances.

Often there's something that can be done about the blues—watching a good movie, taking a drive or a walk, having a conversation with a trusted friend, cleaning a closet, eating chocolate, praying, screaming for two full minutes, reading a good book, exercising, enjoying some music, laughing, or any number of other things.

Depression is a problem of longer duration than the blues—it can be with you daily and can last for a week or much longer. Being down all the time is the main characteristic of depression.

There are also usually physical symptoms associated

with depression. These could include eating or sleeping problems. There is often a loss of interest in things we would usually enjoy. General energy and curiosity are low and fatigue is high.

People who are struggling with real depression usually feel a lot of guilt, helplessness, and hopelessness. The chief thing that separates the blues from depression is a loss, in the latter, of our ability to react positively to surroundings. The truly depressed person isn't going to derive pleasure from even the best or happiest of experiences.

Someone who is clinically depressed is literally in pain. And it's a pain that is very intense. Comparing the blues to depression is like comparing a headache to a migraine.

So I'm sticking with talking about the "blues" right now, and I just pray that those who experience anything more serious will get the help they need.

Have you figured out what makes you feel blue (besides a lack of flowers and sunshine)?

For example, think of how you can feel your mood change (if it does) when it rains . . . when it gets dark at night . . . when the alarm goes off in the morning . . . when the laundry expands, doubling, tripling . . . when you're awfully cold, or awfully hot . . . when your team loses . . . when you have a "bad hair day" . . . when you're driving and you're in a hurry . . . when you get in the slow line . . . when you run out of time . . . when there's too much to do . . . when someone you love is hurting, and you don't know how to help . . .

About twenty-five years ago when I was feeling a bit blue (kind of light blue—not terribly dark), I decided to make up a list of things that could depress me. It was kind of a tongue-in-cheek, "reverse psychology" exercise for me to list a bunch of ideas for how to feel blue:

—Make mountains out of molehills. This is really fun. Think about all you have to do when you're in your most exhausting part of the day.

—Take everything personally. Endeavor to make everything that goes wrong your fault. This takes some skill, but with practice you can do it. I know you can!

—Do as much criticizing as you can, of yourself, your spouse, your kids, your parents, your neighbors, leaders, people in the news, people you don't even know, fictitious people . . . find fault and promote contention.

—Eat all you possibly can. Set goals, like 300 pounds

by the end of the year! Eat things that make you feel tired, give you a headache, or make you sick.

—Plan a ski trip to Las Vegas or a beach vacation in Alice Springs. Maybe a star-gazing week in Manhattan or bird watching in a mall.

—Spend a lot of time dreaming about things that will likely never come true. You as Miss Delaware or Mrs. Canada. Your husband as Mr. Universe. Your children as prodigies of math, ice sculpting, music, astronomy, or Play-Doh.

—Compare yourself to others: your weaknesses to others' strengths. Don't let one person represent more than one or two talents or categories, though—and don't find out too much about them except for the *one* thing in which they are better or more skilled than you are. (If you find out more about them, it may begin to decrease your stress and depression as you find out they have their own struggles and burdens, and they can't do *everything*.)

—A little "variation" on this comparing theme is to compare your strengths to others' weaknesses. It's a little more challenging, but it allows you to get deeper into judging, criticizing, complaining, and murmuring. Great stuff!

—Spend all the money you can. Get a lot of credit

cards (applications will arrive in the mail just when you need them) and get out there to those malls and haul all the stuff away. (Caution: There may be some initial euphoria before the depression sets in, but it'll come!— probably with the bills.)

—Don't plan your day, just let it happen. Be surprised, be shocked, be caught off guard, be frustrated. Don't do the dishes for four or five days. Set fire to the laundry.

—When you feel angry, scream and throw things. Don't stop to figure out *why* you're upset, just let it all out as fast and noisily and publicly and with as much drama as you can. Break things you can't replace, and say and do things that you'll regret and feel embarrassed about later on.

—Think of all the things you don't like about your home or apartment or tent or tree house (wherever it is you live). Name these things, dwell on them, tell yourself nothing is ever going to change.

—Don't sing or whistle or hum or play the piano or any other musical instrument.

—Don't socialize! Lock yourself in your room. Don't call people on the phone. Don't go outside if there's a chance you might run into someone. Don't eat with your family.

—Make a list of all the things you can think of that are awful in the world right now. Add things to the list that are awful in your neighborhood and in your life. Make the list as long as you can. Make copies. Hang them up where you'll see them often. Put the worst things in a 36-point typeface, really *huge*.

—Say yes to everything anyone even hints that they want you to do, whether you'd enjoy it or not, whether you have time or energy for it or not, whether it's something you feel you can do or not. Call up people to get more things to do.

What a stupid list! I can see by your face (even if I'm nowhere near where you're reading) that I've really helped you in your quest to be down.

This little exercise has reminded me of how there are those who want us to be as miserable as they are. I actually don't want to be on that team at all.

I've lived long enough to know what kinds of things bring on the blues for me. Is that true with you too? I say: Stay in the red zone, or the yellow, or green, or fuchsia!

I still have blue as my favorite color, and I still sing

the song about the blues, but I consciously work at limiting my time spent feeling blue. Sometimes all I have to do is say to myself with that certain tone of voice: "Snap out of it!"

My Heavenly Father wants me to be happy, not blue all the time, and I feel a lot better when I pay attention to Him.

Seasoned to Perfection

Before my father went Home (at age ninety-five), I watched him go through many seasons. Although some were exceedingly challenging, he seemed committed to doing his best no matter what his circumstance. Toward the end, I began having the feeling that Dad had been "seasoned to perfection."

Life has a lot of seasons, doesn't it? I love the changes from winter to spring, from summer to fall. I like having all four seasons, with the promise of the next one in the current one.

When I was little, my favorite months all had the letter *u* in them: June, July, August. I loved summers. But I've changed. Now all my favorite months have *r* in them, starting with September.

Our lives have seasons, and perhaps, as with the weather, there are some that seem more enjoyable, productive, interesting, beautiful, or whatever. But if our whole life were our favorite season, we likely wouldn't learn or grow as much. It might even get boring.

How about *your* life—what have your seasons been like so far? Do any of you feel like you're getting close to season 100? Not that you're a hundred years old . . . you could be only thirty and feel like you've had a hundred seasons.

Maybe you're raising children, doing your best to make sure they're happy and healthy, clothed and fed, bright and well-mannered, and so on. Do you receive a lot of advice about how to make it through this season? I hope you have more people who genuinely help rather than just evaluate and judge what and how you're doing.

Maybe this is your season for a demanding Church calling, and if it were the *only* thing you had to do in your life you could really "do a number" on it. But you're doing well—you're praying, studying, preparing, and giving your best. And you're somehow keeping up with all the other things in your life most of the time.

Perhaps you sometimes feel lonely, abandoned, not needed. If that is a season you're experiencing, I pray it won't last long.

Maybe you're in school, and you wonder if you'll ever be finished with tests, and papers to write, and pages to read, and lectures to comprehend. Do you wonder if there will ever be a time when you can read for pleasure again?

Maybe you're serving as a missionary, either as a young person or as a senior missionary. For many, this particular season seems like an oasis, challenging, but beautiful. It might be hard to say yes to a mission, but oh, the incredible experience of representing Jesus Christ wherever He sends you!

Maybe your season is closer to being like my mother's. She says she is so far over the hill she thinks she only dreamed about it!

Mom, who is now over ninety, had a stroke when she was seventy-eight and highly recommends that if you're going to have one of those you should not wait too long. She feels she would have enjoyed her stroke so much more if she'd been younger. She realizes there are things she used to do that she just can't do anymore. (You don't have to be past ninety before you realize there are things you can no longer do, huh?)

Driving a car is one of the most difficult things Mom had to let go of, and it was the same for my father. Maybe for you it will be square dancing or sky diving. Maybe you'll miss being in the rodeo or taking long walks.

My mother lives with my younger brother John, his wife, Melanie, and their six children. Melanie's parents also live there for much of the year, so it's a full and busy household. There are many experiences and sweet blessings that come from having three generations living together.

This family had, for several years, a little pug dog named Ivan. The day came when Ivan was very sick and had to be put to sleep. This was a very difficult thing for the family, especially my mother, who loved the dog and enjoyed the companionship so much. It was also a very difficult thing for nine-year-old Jill. She wrote her feelings down a little while after Ivan died. I share them without having made any corrections.

"IVAN . . . I miss Ivan. He was my best friend. He was my favorite pet of those 7 years.

"He was my favorite pug dog. He had to get put to sleep Mar. 3, 2007 because all his muscles in his body started to hurt each second. There was no medication we could give him to save him from this illness. We couldn't just leave him like this. . . . So we had to put him to sleep.

"So far it has been the most difficult thing so far in my life. I loved him with all my heart.

"If I had the choice I would of taken his spot to die.

I hope that the angels are taking good care of him. I love Ivan and miss him, that's all I got to say."

A little child sharing a sense of loss with her grandmother is a precious, holy thing.

My mother looks back on many interesting seasons—a mother of eight with many grandchildren and great-grandchildren, a nurse, Silver Beaver, self-taught farmer and vet, exceptional cook and gardener, Relief Society president, camp director, and so on.

Your list is just as amazing.

Maybe your season is similar in some ways to mine (although I realize that we're never in *exactly* the same circumstance as anyone else). I'm retired, but I'm as busy as I ever was.

Inside I feel like I could still leap tall buildings, but in reality I can hardly leap dust balls.

I say silly things like, "I'm not as young as I used to be." DUH!

There's that phrase from the book of Luke, describing some of us as "stricken in years" (Luke 1:7). I don't remember when I first discovered that I could no longer take the stairs two or three at a time or run without getting tired. Or run at all. . . . Now I get out of breath just hauling the garbage can out to the street. And it's so much harder these days to get in and out of my pup tent! Am I really the same person who was voted BFA (Best Female Athlete) in my high school about eighty years ago?

Another thing that has changed is my hearing. I take after my dad rather than my mother in that department. A couple of years ago I was on a flight from Salt Lake City to Oakland, California. A man sat beside me who looked like he was a "frequent flyer."

So when he got seated I asked, "Do you fly a lot?"

"I sure do."

I asked what business he was in, and he said, "Books." Oh, that was an *easy* one to respond to! I went on and on about some books I had read recently, telling him how much I'd enjoyed them. Then I asked if he thought people read as much as they used to, and he said he thought they probably did. I asked, "When you travel, are you selling books?" He looked at me with a bit of humor mixed with a sigh and said, "BOATS. B-O-A-T-S. *BOATS.*"

"Oh . . ."

I told the stake Relief Society president and her husband about this experience, and the next day when they took me back to the airport we crossed over the Golden

Gate Bridge and went down near the bay. There were some beautiful boats out on the water, and one was really huge. The husband said, "Wow—that's a pretty big book!"

It wasn't long after that trip that I got my hearing aids.

I never thought it would be my turn to notice these little surprises of nature, these saggings and malfunctions, the slowing down and suchlike. These days it takes twice as long to look half as good. I find myself humming "Have I Done Any Good in the World Today" a little more often than I used to. I'm still looking forward most of the time, but I also find I look back more than I did when I was twenty or thirty.

As I've been thinking about all of this, I've decided that many seasons overlap. Several might descend on us at once. We think spring has come, but there's another "cold snap." We think summer will be long and hot, and all of a sudden it's time to harvest the apples, roll up the hoses, and carve the pumpkins.

Each age, each season, has lessons and satisfaction that can be known only by experience. What have your seasons taught you? Have they helped to bring insight, compassion, faith, patience, perspective, and other qualities of soul? Are we getting all we can out of each of our seasons?

Sometimes we try to deny our age, or mask the signs of aging. Many observers feel that this is a great obstacle to aging gracefully.

There are challenges in growing older, yes, but there are also many benefits. I saw on the Internet this list of perks of being over sixty-five:

—Kidnappers are not very interested in you.
—There is nothing left to learn the hard way.
—Most things you buy now won't wear out.
—You can quit trying to hold your stomach in.
—Your investment in health insurance is actually finally beginning to pay off.
—Your supply of brain cells is finally down to a manageable size.

Other benefits of growing older include increased wisdom, a wonderful depth of character, a collection of extraordinary memories, and the ability to let go of things that don't matter and focus on the things that matter most. And you can finally let go of activities more suited to younger bodies. As Golda Meir said, "Being seventy is not a sin."

Think of the average age of the fifteen men whom we sustain as prophets, seers, and revelators! Okay, I'm not a math major, but I figure it's somewhere around seventy-five. President Hinckley, at age ninety-seven, really affects those numbers, doesn't he? These fifteen men have more than 1,100 combined years of life experience! We are in good hands!

Aging is not a sudden event, it's a process. And there just is not a way to grow younger, is there? The fountain of youth is a *myth* . . . except that I think I found a recipe that comes pretty close:

"For the natural man is an enemy to God, and has been from the fall of Adam, and will be, forever and ever, unless he yields to the enticings of the Holy Spirit, and putteth off the natural man and becometh a saint through the atonement of Christ the Lord, and becometh as a child, submissive, meek, humble, patient, full of love, willing to submit to all things which the Lord seeth fit to inflict upon him, even as a child doth submit to his father" (Mosiah 3:19).

We mortals will all eventually die. The goal isn't to live forever—the goal is to create and invest in something that *will!* And along the way we need to value each other not just for what we can do, but for who we are.

I've interviewed several women to get their take on this whole issue of aging. Verrrrrry interesting! This may surprise you, but I got an e-mail from Mary Methuselah. (Write *that* in your journal! "Edmunds got an email from Methuselah's wife!") Her friends called her Muffy. Here are some excerpts from her e-mail:

"So you're talking about aging, are you? Well, I lived almost thirty years after my husband died (at age 969), so that takes me pretty near having lived 1,000 years. And you think 100 years is a big deal! Ha ha. Try adding another zero! You think *you're* old? My husband was a 'boy' of 100 when Adam himself ordained him to the priesthood. Did you know my husband was an astronomer? Lots of people don't know that. By the way, *his* nickname was "Meth," and I think he'd have had to change it if he lived now. Life on earth was pretty interesting for me. We didn't worry about things like cholesterol or road rage . . . nor did we have manicures, Botox, or tummy tucks. Those I don't think I'd have missed even if I'd known about them.

"But *oh,* to have indoor plumbing and electricity! I have to say that I really loved my father-in-law, Enoch, even though it took me a few days to get over being left behind when he and his city were taken to heaven. My husband helped me realize that it was on purpose—that he and I both needed to keep teaching what our parents had taught. Our grandson Noah became quite famous— you've probably heard of him. He only lived to be 950. Did you know he was around 600 years old when he finished building the ark? And you think you're too old to be a Scout leader or a Laurel advisor! Can you imagine being 500 years old before you have a midlife crisis? So don't talk to any of *us* about getting old . . . just enjoy your experiences and do your best."

I'm so grateful to Muffy Methuselah for that wonderful e-mail message.

To me, there is a difference between aging (a very natural phenomenon that happens to all of us) and growing old. Thus, I have come up with some alternatives to growing old:

Growing happy . . . grateful . . . content.

Growing wise . . . and kind . . . and endurable. Yes, endurable! Able to endure to the end! (Plus, it kind of sounds like *adorable,* and that's another good alternative to growing old: growing adorable!)

Some who reach retirement age seem to feel, "I've done my share. Now it's someone else's turn." But withdrawing can actually hasten the aging process.

What if President Hinckley had decided to "retire" at age sixty-five? Or seventy-five. Or even eighty-five or ninety-five! Thank goodness he didn't! Just think: If he had retired at age sixty-five, we would have missed more than thirty years of his goodness, his leadership, his humor, his faith, his counsel.

The Savior increased in wisdom and stature and in favor with God and man—and so can we. We still have a lot of living to do.

You're never too old and it's never too late to keep learning. My friend Florence Richards used to choose one new thing to learn each year. One year it was how to play the accordion. She told me she found someone in the ward who had one in her attic. By Christmastime Florence could play "Lady of Spain" pretty well.

What is it *you* do to keep learning—to keep your mind active and busy? Maybe you work on crafts or crossword puzzles. Maybe you read or keep a journal. Some aging people challenge themselves with trying to remember the names of their children and grandchildren . . . or they go overboard and try to remember spouses and birthdays! That'll keep your brain busy!

You're never too old and it's never too late to live each day with purpose and enthusiasm. I love seeing older people who still have passion for the things that matter most to them. (And by this time they should have a pretty good idea of what matters most!)

You're never too old and it's never too late to give things away. Do this while you can still remember why you've saved some of your treasures—why they mean so much. You can explain that as you give these treasures to someone you love.

You're never too old to dream dreams, to serve, to remember, to be cheerful, to do some exercising of both body and mind.

You're never too old to reach out to those in need, to smile, to be a happifier.

You're never too old to keep covenants, to communicate openly and honestly with Heavenly Father, to become more Christlike and Godlike.

President Gordon B. Hinckley shared the following: "To you older women and men who are widows and widowers, how precious you are. You have lived long and had much of experience. You have tasted the bitter and the sweet. You have known much of pain and sorrow and loneliness and fear. But you also carry in your hearts a sweet and sublime assurance that God our Father will not fail us in our hour of need. May the years that lie ahead be kind to you. May heaven smile upon you. May you draw comfort and strength from your memories. And may you, with your mature kindness and love, reach out to help those in distress wherever you find them" (*Ensign,* March 1997, 63).

That's beautiful, isn't it?

Some of us may have feelings similar to those recorded in Psalm 71, verses 7 and 9: "I am as a wonder unto many; but thou art my strong refuge. . . . Cast me not off in the time of old age; forsake me not when my strength faileth."

There will *never* come a time when your Heavenly Father forgets about you. There's not some policy in heaven where they turn you loose when you turn seventy. "She can't move fast enough anymore to get into trouble, so focus on the young 'uns."

To echo President Hinckley: May the years that lie ahead be kind to you. May heaven smile upon you in every season of your life!

Saying Good-bye

I've never written out a list of things I'd like to accomplish in my life, at least not one that came close to being like author John Goddard's list. A kayak down the Nile? I don't think so!

But I *have* had a few things in my mind that I've wanted to see or accomplish. Included on my informal list were things like learning another language (I grew up pretty fluent in English and Pig Latin), digging a tunnel to China (the Lombardi brothers got a whole lot closer than I did, and they even let me spend some time in their tunnel), playing my violin in the *Messiah* (thank goodness everyone got to participate in Cedar City . . . if there had been tryouts I don't know if I ever would have made it), becoming a nurse (it happened), becoming a mother (I'm not married and I've not had any children, but I feel like I've done a lot of mothering, a lot of nurturing), writing a book (you're holding one), teaching (one of my greatest joys), seeing the Statue of Liberty (a deeply emotional experience), and so on.

Further down the list was the chance to attend something in Carnegie Hall in New York City, and I got to do that with my friend Carol. I wasn't exactly comfortable in that huge hall—I felt like I was at the top of a roller-coaster ride just before the 75-foot fall, only I didn't know when it was going to fall.

Still, I loved the concert by Marilyn Horne. What a voice, even at that stage of her career (her peak performances were behind her). For one of her encore numbers she sang "Bridge Over Troubled Waters." Oh my goodness—it was so beautiful and so moving!

Another of her encores was something I had never heard before, but I found it especially meaningful. She had asked a composer friend to set to music a poem, "Never More," about someone who had gone on. It was tender and so very, very meaningful.

I thought of this in connection with my dear Daddy going Home. I'd like to share a little bit about it. He was ninety-five years old and had lived a great life, a wonderful life. He'd wanted to live to be a hundred, and he almost made it. He lived for most of a century, and from

1902 to 1997 he had seen a *lot* of things happen in the world.

In those last days of his life he came home from the hospital for Christmas, and it was a fantastic day. All eight of us children were gathered around him and our mother. Almost all thirty grandchildren were there too, and eleven great-grandchildren.

With the miracle of a little "pocket-talker" gadget we all had chances to tell him Merry Christmas, to report on Christmas morning, to ask questions and hear his wonderful answers. Little ones looked into his bright blue eyes as they sang about "Rudolph," told him what Santa had brought, and gave him their special Christmas gifts and greetings. No visit from Santa Claus could have come close to the feeling of having Dad right where he belonged for this particular Christmas Day.

The next day it seemed that Christmas had been almost too much for him. He was pretty much "zonked" the whole day and not responding much to anyone who visited him. But on Saturday, December 27, he was once again with us, as bright and alert as ever, and most of us had the chance to visit him that day.

I was there for a while in the afternoon, and it seemed he didn't want me to leave. Did he have some idea of what was coming? I think perhaps he did. He welcomed me so warmly. I talked to him, hugged him, got him water to drink, and tried to adjust his bed to where he felt comfortable. He was so sweet as he'd ask, "Try it a little bit higher," and I'd crank it a little bit (the bed didn't have the electrical way of being raised and lowered), wanting to make it "just right." Almost apologetically he'd say, "Maybe a little lower."

When I finally did leave, just as my sister Charlotte and her daughter were coming, he said, as always, "Thank you for your visit." Always the perfect gentleman and gentle man.

Early on Saturday evening, shortly after my sister Ann and her two boys had left, something drastic happened to Dad, and with his many years of experience as a physician he knew exactly when, and he knew exactly what.

There was a rupture in the intestine with the inevitable excruciating pain.

Dad was taken to the emergency room, and all of us began to gather. It was time for our Daddy to leave us. Surgery was not an option. All eight of us gathered and had a family prayer. We told him how much we loved him, how much we would miss him, and we promised to take good care of our mother. We told Dad to say hello to loved ones.

Here we all were, sealed together because of the covenants of our patriarch, our precious father, who now needed to leave us for a little while. We could sense how much it meant to him to have all of us there, especially his sweetheart, his favorite nurse, our mother.

We all took turns sitting by Dad, holding his hand and talking to him. A grandchild read scriptures to him. A great-grandchild sang "I Am a Child of God." One little one who wasn't there called the hospital on the telephone to ask her dad, "Is Grandpa still alive?" "Yes, Tina." "Does he still love me?" "Oh, yes."

We noticed that his blood pressure was slowly but surely going down.

I know Dad was listening to us, aware of our love and tender feelings. He'd squeeze our hands as we held his. We wanted to make sure we were always touching him—that he always knew we were right there—that he wasn't alone. He certainly *wasn't* alone, and I'm not just talking about "earthlings."

We spoke of those who would be waiting for Dad, including his own dear father, whom he had not seen since he was nine years old, and his mother, and his brothers and sisters.

At 3:00 P.M. everyone had gone except for me and Charlotte. Others had left to care for their children, to rest, to prepare to spend the night back at the hospital. We were preparing to be beside Dad in shifts, at least two at a time. If we had known what would happen next, no one would have left.

Almost the moment everyone had gone except the two of us, Dad's breathing changed. Charlotte noticed it first, and looked over at me and said, "He's going!" We knew it, but we didn't want it to be true. We hugged and kissed our sweet Daddy, and I kept asking, "Are you going, Daddy? Is it time for you to go?"

Charlotte leaned over and said, "You can go, Daddy—you can go now."

I think that was what he needed to know—that it was all right for him to respond to the angelic beckoning of which he most certainly was aware.

We kept talking to him. I promised him again that we'd take good care of Mom.

It was about 3:20 on that Sunday afternoon when he didn't breathe anymore. Quietly, tenderly, gently, our Daddy slipped away from us.

Is there anything more sacred or holy than hugging your Daddy as he slips from your loving arms to those of his own Daddy and Mother, brothers and sisters, Savior and Heavenly Parents?

Now, fast forward a couple of months. I had been asked to write a chapter for a Christmas book titled *I'll Be Home for Christmas.* I needed to get it sent to the publisher by February of 1998. But I just couldn't seem to get going on it. I had the title: "Coming Home, Going Home." But I just couldn't make the words come.

Then, one *early* morning in February, right around 2:30, I was awakened by something. I felt I could hear Dad's voice in my mind and heart saying something like, "Sweetie, get up and turn on your computer. Let's write a chapter."

For several hours I typed and wept, typed and wept, and the chapter "happened." It was such a tender and comforting (even healing) time for me. It was as if my Dad was right beside me, helping me and letting me know he was all right.

I would type for a while and then start sobbing. So much of my grief came out on that early winter's morning while my Daddy was very close to me. I'd walk around the house sobbing uncontrollably and letting my anguish and loneliness and sorrow come out freely. And then I'd get back to the computer and continue typing until it was time to walk around again. What an incredibly sweet experience I had with my Dad!

I had other experiences during that year, but one of the sweetest happened several months later, on Christmas Eve. During the day I was sitting in my "Christmas Room" wrapping some gifts and whistling. (I whistle a lot when I'm alone.)

I was feeling homesick for Dad. Tears would come off and on as I thought about him. I really, really missed my Daddy.

At some point I had a strong impression, as if I could hear the Holy Ghost speaking to me in my mind. "What are you whistling?" "Oh, it's some Primary song." "Which one?" "The one about Father." "What are the words? Say them out loud."

And then I did (and this wasn't a Primary song I learned when I was in Primary, and I've never worked in Primary, but somehow I know this one). "I know my Father lives and loves me too. The Spirit whispers this to me and tells me it is true, And tells me it is true" (*Hymns,* no. 302). Can you imagine the *comfort* I received as I sat weeping, knowing this message was sent from two

Fathers Up There? They both knew how much I needed such a message on that Christmas Eve a year after Dad went Home.

One year after my father died, on the last Sunday of 1998, I felt like I wanted to at least drive past the hospital where I last saw him alive (in the earthly sense only).

I got there and was filled with sweet feelings about him and what had happened just a year before. I decided I would just drive into the emergency entrance parking area. Then I decided to park the car. I was kind of in "slow motion," and everything was quiet around me.

Next I decided maybe I'd just go inside. As I opened the car door, there was a penny on the ground. I laughed softly, feeling like Dad had put it there. I said out loud, "Yes, Dad, I still pick up pennies." It was kind of a private signal between us of our awareness of being careful and frugal. I still have that penny sitting in my car where I can see it.

Next I thought I'd just walk past the ER. I ended up walking all the way down the hall to the elevators. So I thought I might as well go up to the 6th floor. Once I got there I thought maybe I'd just go over to where Dad had been—Room 617.

As I got closer, I was continuing to feel isolated from

everyone—as if no one could see me. I wasn't interrupted in any way. I thought maybe I'd just poke my head in the room, and if someone was in there I'd apologize and leave.

No one was in the room. There wasn't even a bed in there. So I went in and spent some time. It was about the same hour as it had been the year before when Charlotte and I had been with Dad and he had gone Home. I talked to him. It was a comforting and unusual experience.

Later I told my brothers and sisters that the room was empty, just as the tomb was empty, and Dad is as alive as any of us and is involved in things that really, really matter.

And so I can hear Marilyn Horne singing her song, "Never More," and I can say to her and anyone else that yes, as far as things on this earth are concerned, never more will we see him here. But he is still a light in our heart, and he is gone, but not far. We'll be with him again. This I know. This I really, really know.

The Flight to Rexburg

It was "double ten" day in 1986: 10 October. I've always remembered that it's an important Chinese holiday, this "double ten" day. And this is one that will stand out in my mind forever because of what I experienced.

I had planned to go to Rexburg, Idaho, for the inauguration of Joe J. Christensen as president of Ricks College. He'd actually been there for about a year, but his inauguration was delayed because of the death of President Spencer W. Kimball.

I had planned to drive, but my friends Joy and Dave said, "Why not go with us? We're flying." That sounded like an adventure, and even though I'm afraid of small planes, I thought about all the time I would save and how enjoyable it would be to travel with Dave and Joy, so I agreed.

We were out at the Salt Lake airport in plenty of

time, but somehow the friend with the airplane was late coming. But we all climbed in—Dave in front as co-pilot, and Joy and I sitting in the other two seats right behind the men. And off we went.

It was my first time in such a small plane, and I quite enjoyed the chance to see so much of what was on the ground. It was hard to visit, though, as the noise of the propeller drowned out all but shouting.

As I was looking at everything, I realized at some point that we were passing Ricks College.

"Hey," I hollered. Not loud enough. No response. "Hey, there's Rexburg! There's Ricks!" Joy heard me and shouted at Dave and the pilot.

They didn't think it could be Rexburg. The pilot shouted back something about according to his calculations we had several more miles to go.

I shouted, "But there's Ricks. There's the stadium right down there. And the Hart and Manwaring buildings."

The pilot shouted, "Are you sure?"

Yes, I was sure. I even pointed out the little airport back behind us. I had noticed it as we flew over.

Finally he believed me. He circled, found the air strip, and landed.

We knew we were late, and we were in a hurry. Dave rushed into a tiny office and said, "What's the best way for us to get to the college?" The woman on duty said, "Take my car—it's the old one out there, and the key's in it." She didn't even ask our names or how long we'd be gone!

We missed a lot of what happened but had a wonderful time anyway, and all too soon it was over and time to go back home.

When we got back to the airport, the wind had picked up and was blowing pretty hard. The little plane bounced around all the way back to Salt Lake, and I was terrified—absolutely terrified. It was like a combination of the five most frightening amusement-park rides you've ever been on in your life. I think I still have scars where I dug my fingernails into the palms of my hands. Once the engine even conked out! I knew I was going to die! But the pilot just calmly started it again and we continued flying (a.k.a. bouncing) south.

I've thought a lot about that experience, and about flight plans and staying on course and all.

A pilot has to submit a flight plan before he or she takes off. Without a plan, how would there be any chance of reaching a destination? Without navigational instruments and communication helps, how would a pilot know for sure if he or she were on course? Especially if it were cloudy, or if the plane were over water.

Amelia Earhart made plans to fly completely around the globe in 1937. She had flown across the continent and was a very experienced, competent aviator. She left Miami on June 1. She went across South America, Africa, and Asia. She and her navigator reached New Guinea and then took off for Howland Island, somewhere out in the Pacific.

On that day, there was rain and fog, and the Coast Guard picked up a frantic message from Amelia: "Cannot hear you . . . please take a bearing on us and answer . . ."

There was trouble with the radio. Her final transmission was "Circling . . . cannot see island . . . gas is running low . . . running north and south . . ." And then silence (see David R. Collins, "First Lady of the Sky," *Friend*, June 1975, 37).

Somehow the little plane had gotten off course, and it was lost, along with its two passengers.

Life can be like that. There's a plan—the Great Plan of Happiness—but there is also a lot of opposition (storms, turbulence, darkness, strong head winds, and other things) trying to take us off course. We need to make course corrections every bit as much as a pilot in a plane.

Elder L. Tom Perry has flown a lot in his life, and he said he's been fascinated by looking in the cockpit at all the instruments and controls. He tells of a particular conversation with a pilot:

"I entered into a discussion with one pilot regarding what could happen if he deviated from his flight plan. I proposed deviating just one degree from the charted course. His reply astonished me. He said that for every one-degree variance from the plan, you would miss your charted destination by one mile for every 60 miles you were flying. . . .

"On a flight from Salt Lake to Chicago, you would miss the airport and land in Lake Michigan. Going from Salt Lake to New York, you would miss Kennedy Airport and land in the Hudson River. Going to London, you wouldn't even make England—you would land somewhere in France. . . .

"The pilot explained to me that, obviously, the faster the error is discovered, the easier it is to return to the flight plan. . . . My visit with the pilot . . . [caused] me to think of how a flight plan parallels the direction we chart for our life's experience" (*Ensign,* August 1996, 10).

I think about how much more effective the Holy Ghost is in our lives than any kind of gauges or navigational instruments, or even an air traffic controller. There is really no comparison or substitute—but there is a very good analogy.

Our lives can be aimless without a plan. As Yogi Berra reportedly said, "You got to be careful if you don't know where you're going, because you might not get there." Uh, yes . . .

Am I on course? Am I headed where I really want to go?

Do you find it's important to think about it—to analyze how your journey is coming?

I think about these things a lot, and I aim to do all I can to have a "happy landing."

Laugh with MEE

For a few years at the Missionary Training Center I oversaw the work of those learning American Sign Language. One day their supervisor brought her group to my office door to announce they'd been asked to sing at the MTC Christmas program. I could tell something funny was about to happen by the look on her face.

"Do you want to know what they've chosen to sing?" she asked.

"Of course I do!" I responded, noticing that the missionaries were watching closely for my reaction.

"Our two numbers are 'Do You Hear What I Hear?' and 'I Heard Him Come.'"

I cracked up! And the missionaries, several of whom were deaf, laughed and clapped.

I'm convinced that we are born with happy, cheerful,

sunny, optimistic dispositions—that it is part of our heritage from our Heavenly Father.

Heber C. Kimball helped me understand this. He said: "I am perfectly satisfied that my Father and my God is a cheerful, pleasant, lively, and good-natured Being. Why? Because I am cheerful, pleasant, lively, and good-natured when I have His Spirit" (*Journal of Discourses,* 4:222).

Has that been your experience? As you have felt the Spirit, have you also felt joy? I know that feeling joy and happiness doesn't mean we're always laughing our heads off. Although . . . laughter is very healing.

President James E. Faust told students at Brigham Young University: "Don't forget to laugh at the silly things that happen. Humor . . . is a powerful force for good when used with discretion. Its physical expression, laughter, is highly therapeutic" (*Church News,* November 22, 1997).

That is true. When we laugh hard, our heart rate speeds up, the circulatory and immune systems are stimulated, and more endorphins are produced. (And then they go perform at Sea World!)

A few Septembers ago, my mother went with me to St. George for a women's conference. This was during the annual St. George Senior Games, and as we shuffled into the motel—Mom leaning on her walker and me dragging our luggage—we noticed all the shipshape senior athletes. I said to her, "Hey, Mom, they think we're here for the Senior Games! They're wondering what our sport is!" We laughed so hard that our forward progress stopped for several minutes.

I'm so grateful for what I have learned from my parents about being cheerful, lighthearted, and—yes—sometimes silly.

Sister Marjorie Hinckley had (and I'm sure still has) a delightful sense of humor. She said: "The only way to get through life is to laugh your way through it. You either have to laugh or cry. I prefer to laugh. Crying gives me a headache" (Virginia H. Pearce, ed., *Glimpses into the Life and Heart of Marjorie Pay Hinckley* [Deseret Book, 1999], 107).

One time I had what I thought was a very clever idea. I was on a mission in the Philippines, and we had an abundance of tiny little bugs and critters there—ants, fleas, bedbugs, termites, mosquitoes, flies, and baby cockroaches. I got some clear tape, and I would put a variety of all these little critters on the tape and make what I thought was a very unusual, attractive "letterhead."

I began sending these letters to everyone, knowing they would feel cheered up and cherished. I even sent one of these letterhead pieces of homemade stationery to the General Authority assigned to our area, who happened to be Elder Gordon B. Hinckley.

The next time Sister Hinckley came with her husband to the Philippines, she had a surprise for me. In Asia we often had a treat called Smarties, kind of like M&Ms, which came in a cardboard tube similar to one that would hold pens or pencils.

When Sister Hinckley arrived, with a happy smile she gave me one of these Smartie tubes. Inside the tube I found a lively little lizard—a gecko!

Somehow I realized that Sister Hinckley wanted to help us cut down on our "bug and critter" population in our little place in the Philippines. (Maybe she was also saying that one of those "critter letters" was enough.) I loved the good humor with which she handled that interaction!

President Gordon B. Hinckley said: "We need to have a little humor in our lives. We better take seriously that which should be taken seriously, but at the same time we can bring in a touch of humor now and again. If the time ever comes when we can't smile at ourselves, it will be a sad time" (interview with *Church News,* September 1, 1995).

We do need to take seriously that which should be taken seriously, and President Hinckley has always done that. But he has also helped us laugh together, and laugh at ourselves, in such happy ways.

Certainly not everything is funny. I know that. Someone who tells jokes all the time—to whom *everything* is funny—does *not* have a sense of humor, in my opinion. And if we hurt someone's feelings, it's not funny.

But a good sense of humor seems to me to be a way to keep from being too pretentious, too perfectionistic, or too isolated or insulated from others. It's a kind of honesty in looking at ourselves and all that surrounds us.

Often my own humor seems to be an acknowledgment of my weaknesses, and thus a way to help me continue striving to do better and be better. It's a way for me to be *real,* to be genuine and honest in sharing my thoughts and feelings with others. It helps me avoid something I have earnestly sought to stay away from: hypocrisy.

So I try to laugh at myself whenever the opportunity presents itself.

Several years ago on Easter weekend I had assignments to speak in Fresno and Visalia (California). In order to save at least $7.00, I flew into Sacramento rather than Fresno. This allowed me the opportunity to drive to Fresno in the traffic of not just any Friday afternoon, but "Good Friday" afternoon.

I had made arrangements to go to the Fresno Temple with Lynn, whom I'd met at a women's conference in the area a few years earlier. When I finally got to the motel in Fresno and called her, I admit I was hoping she'd say that she wouldn't be there for another ten minutes or so. But no, she was very close, so I just said that I would hurry and change and meet her in the lobby.

I changed and collected my things as quickly as I could and headed back for the lobby, smiling and waving at the people who were in the halls and those cleaning the rooms.

I got to the lobby and met Lynn, and I smiled and waved at the kind people at the desk who had helped me check in just a few minutes earlier.

We got into the car, and I was buckling my seat belt when I noticed, to my *horror,* that I had forgotten my skirt!

I couldn't believe it! It just was *not there* where it should have been! I had on a slip, but it definitely *looked* like a slip . . . it looked *nothing* like a skirt!

So I said to Lynn, "I forgot my skirt!" And she said something like, "Oh, I didn't notice."

What? How could you *not* notice something like that! I wanted to do my grade-school rendition of "Liar, liar, pants on fire . . ." Instead, I said, "I'd better go get my skirt, since we're going to the temple." She agreed.

Back into the motel I went, smiling and waving . . .

I'm just here to tell you that sometimes dreams DO come true! Believe it!

I read a sweet account in an *Ensign* magazine several years ago. A mother who was diagnosed with cancer told of being isolated in a bare room for many long days behind closed, lead-lined doors, feeling like a prisoner convicted of a crime she didn't commit.

Then she tells of her oldest daughter coming to visit. "She sat down behind the lead screen that separated us and proceeded to take off her boots and socks. She slipped her socks on her hands and pretended they were puppets and spoke through them. I laughed for the first time in months. That simple act brightened my outlook instantly" (Emily Farmer, *Ensign,* April 1990, 73).

I know there's a difference between lightheartedness and lightmindedness. I've done a *lot* of thinking about the difference.

I think lightmindedness is *thoughtless* (literally, without thought). It is empty, meaningless, and wasteful. Often there is hypocrisy and scorn associated with lightminded laughter. It is irreverent and unholy. It separates us from the Spirit. The things we talk and laugh about don't encourage, cheer, or edify.

Lightheartedness, on the other hand, is like joyful goodness. It includes all that blesses and happifies us and others. It's being of good cheer while focusing on the things that matter. It's a virtue.

Brother Truman Madsen shares the following:

"Listen to Heber C. Kimball. He is praying with his family and in the midst of the prayer says, 'Father, bless Brother So-and-So.' Then he bursts into a loud laugh. I can imagine the heads of his children popping up and their eyes opening. There is a slight pause, and then he says, 'Lord, it makes me laugh to pray about some people,' and he goes on with his prayer. (See *Life of Heber C. Kimball* p. 427.) I leave you to say whether that is lightmindedness or profound intimacy with the Lord. He knows. We have a funny bone. He gave it to us" (*The Radiant Life* [Bookcraft, 1994], 6).

I remember a time in the Tabernacle years ago on a day when it was *hot.* Everyone was fanning themselves with whatever they could find. President Hinckley got up and said something like, "It's hot in here. We know you're hot. . . . But you're not as hot as you're going to be if you don't repent!" The laughter was instant and joyful.

President Hinckley has been like a visual aid for me in learning about true humor. We really *are* happy people! We can't help it! We know too much! We are like the Nephites—we live "after the manner of happiness" (2 Nephi 5:27).

Elder Neal A. Maxwell points this out in a profound way: "Ultimate hope and daily grumpiness are not reconcilable. It is ungraceful, unjustified, and unbecoming of us as committed Church members to be constantly grumpy or of woeful countenance" (*The Neal A. Maxwell Quote Book* [Bookcraft, 1997], 164).

Have you ever laughed so hard you cried? Somehow there is a close link between tears and laughter. Both bring us so much closer together as friends and fellow travelers. I've felt many times that if I didn't think of a reason to laugh when I'm speaking (teaching), I'd be weeping, and I can't talk very well when I'm weeping.

Elder James E. Talmage said that "[Happiness] springs from the deeper fountains of the soul, and is not infrequently accompanied by tears. Have you never

been so happy that you have had to weep? I have"
(*Improvement Era,* December 1913, 173). We have too,
haven't we?

Good humor helps us hang on and hang in through
the normal ups and downs of life: through paper cuts and
budget cuts, dark and stormy nights, losing at Monopoly
and losing at love, weight gains and heart pains, falling
arches and a falling stock market, flat tires and flat chests,
broken hearts and broken glasses, days when time flies
too quickly and nights when time drags too slowly,
smashed thumbs and hopes, slipping on the ice in front
of two or fifty or a hundred people, spilled jam and traffic jams, and divorce and cancer and single parenthood
and . . . and almost *anything* and *everything.*

Humor can help us avoid constant murmuring and
complaining. Good humor is often the opposite of anger,
envy, and self-centeredness. A humorless heart is too
often a hard heart and leads to a stiff neck. Ouch!

Humor has a way of leveling—of helping us to experience equality. When the same thing touches us or
amuses us, our shared response reaches across a lot of artificial walls and even cuts through language or other communication barriers. I remember in many places where I
couldn't speak the language I seemed still to be able to

communicate, especially with the children, through humor. I'd pull faces and act silly, and we'd laugh and hug each other and feel very, very close.

Let's thank God in the coming days for all there is to be happy about and all that gives us genuine reasons to smile together, to laugh together, to rejoice!

Promotional Videos

My mother used to haunt me by assuring me that the angels in heaven were putting on film every moment of my life, and that someday *everyone* would have a chance to see my "movie." AGH!

I didn't believe her until I started paying attention to the words of the hymn "Do What Is Right" (*Hymns,* no. 237). It's right there in the first verse: "Angels above us are silent notes taking / Of ev'ry action; then do what is right!" What a chilling thought—not to you, maybe, but it sure is to MEE!

Once I did have a little movie made of a personal experience. My friend Jayne had invited me to tell her of a time when I felt close to the Savior, and I shared an experience I'd had in a refugee camp in Thailand in 1981.

It was a Monday in July, and as I spent time walking around the camp, meeting people and observing, I noticed a little girl watching me. She had an oversized pink shirt on. I have no idea how old she was or even who she was. Every time I would try to look directly at her to smile or communicate in some way, she would run away.

As time went by, I was deeply moved by watching and being aware of her. She began to represent everyone in the camp—especially all the little children—and what they'd been through. I wondered a lot about her, who she was, and what she'd had to experience at her tender age.

Toward the end of the day I had gone back to the place where the sister missionaries had their office, and I was sitting leaning on the window with my back to the outside. I had my arms stretched out, and my hand was on the edge of the windowsill.

After a while I noticed the little girl in the pink shirt approaching me, walking very quietly, watching to see if I would turn around. I didn't. I decided just to sit quietly and see what happened.

She got closer and closer, being ever so careful. When she was right next to me she stopped, and we were both very quiet. I didn't turn.

Then she reached up, touched me, and *ran*. It was like electricity—that quick touch on my hand from a tiny finger. I felt it deep in my soul and was moved to tears.

I sat there thinking and feeling, and then I noticed that she was coming back. I still didn't turn, but waited to see what would happen.

Again she approached carefully and quietly, and again she stood waiting. Once again she reached up and touched my hand and then ran. I felt such a tender, powerful response deep inside my heart and soul.

She did this one more time and I still didn't turn, because I still didn't want her to run away afraid.

I guess she finally decided I was dead or something, because she came back. This last time, she stood as she had before, but then she reached up and put her whole small hand on top of mine and pressed it hard and just held it there.

I wept. Oh, I cried so hard! I felt so much love for that child. I wanted something significant to go from me to her. I wanted her to know that she was safe, that I would never do anything to hurt her. I wanted her to feel loved.

I kept thinking, "Oh, little child, *who are you?* Where are you from? Are your parents alive? Do you have any brothers and sisters? Are there people who care about you and are helping you? Where will you go? Where will you live?"

And now I'll go back to the day when I shared this experience with Jayne. We were in a recording studio, but I didn't realize we were being taped until I finished sharing and she looked toward a booth and said, "Did you get it?"

Then she explained that she'd been asked to gather a few experiences to be videotaped for a general Relief Society meeting in the Tabernacle in September of that year, 1985.

Later she called and said the director wanted to meet me. Okay. No problem. He asked me to tell him the experience again, which I did. He had me turn this way and that, and I became aware that he was trying to decide whether I could take the part of MEE in the little reenactment film. (I think that's kind of funny.)

He didn't made a decision then, but he said he would like to have me meet the child they had chosen to take the part of the little girl in the pink shirt, which I did a few days later. I immediately loved Chuum, a Cambodian girl about six or seven years old. She was a little older than the little girl in the camp in Thailand, but she was a refugee herself and hadn't been in America very long. I played with her and her older sister while we waited for the director to be available to talk to me some more.

What I didn't realize (there were quite a few instances of "I didn't realize" in this whole experience) was that he wanted to see how I would interact with Chuum. He seemed pleased, so when he came to talk to me, he asked, "Well, do you think you could play yourself?" Ha. How do you answer a question like that? I told him I would do my best, but that it was more important to me to have the story told well than to be in the film.

Eventually he did choose to have me play my part. It was a fascinating experience. We were at Camp Williams in the Salt Lake Valley, and they had done an incredible job of making a little section of it into a refugee camp. And they had gathered many refugee families—new Americans—to come and participate.

It took the whole day to make the film, and while they were setting things up and shooting other scenes, Chuum and I spent time together. At one point we were sitting in my car, and she was pretending to drive. She asked, "Where we go?"

I said, "Where would you like to go?"

"Disneyland."

"Okay, let's drive to Disneyland."

She was pretending to steer, and we chatted about this and that. I was impressed with how much English she had learned in such a short time.

Then she suddenly stopped steering and looked out the window with concern. She said, "Police!" I couldn't help wondering what she meant by that, and why she seemed so frightened. I wondered what experiences she'd had in her short, unusual life that might make her so afraid of police.

I asked, "Are they coming to the car?" She said they were. I said, "Well, just tell them we're going to Disneyland and see what they say." She did just that and it seemed that everything turned out all right, because she kept steering.

When they filmed the scene where she approached me to touch my hand, I fell to pieces. The whole experience came back as if I were having it again. I couldn't quit crying, because the questions I had asked inside my heart for the little girl in the pink shirt were the same for precious Chuum.

Just as it was four years earlier, I felt so much love for that child. I wanted something significant to go from me to her. I wanted her to know that she was safe, and that I would never do anything to hurt her. I wanted her to feel loved. And I asked some of the very same questions: "Oh, little Chuum, are you all right? Are there people who care about you and are helping you? Where will you go? What will happen to you?"

This little film, about eight minutes long, is now more than twenty years old. And the actual experience upon which it was based happened in 1981. But it is still so fresh in my mind. Is that the way it will be when we are in a position to look back at our lives someday?

I got to thinking again about what my mother had said when I was little (in her attempt to help me improve my behavior). My imagination took off, as it does so very often. What if we had to have a "promotional video" to get into heaven? It would be kind of like a resume, only it would all be on film. Actually, it would more likely be a DVD or some technological marvel even more amazing.

So, the way I picture it, you get to a certain point in the process, and they stick your DVD in a heavenly machine and your video comes on the big screen. Yikes!

This brought a couple of additional thoughts and questions to my mind. For example: Can we edit our videos?

Once, when I was thinking a lot about this, I tried that, just in my mind. I thought of what I would include in a "promotional video" of my life. Naturally, I chose only those things that I thought would give a positive look at my life . . . so I had to edit out a lot. I'm thinking the final cut was about 7½ minutes long. Not a good sign, eh?

I decided, by the way, that editing this promotional video might be sort of like repenting and forgiving—making needed changes.

May we keep the angels in heaven busy recording our quiet kindness, our good deeds, our sincere efforts to do what Jesus would do as we try to become more like Him.

Feasting on the Scriptures

Have you ever been to Las Vegas or any other place where they have those incredible all-you-can-eat buffet feasts? Have you ever wished you could do that once a week or so and then not have to take time to eat again in between? But no, we usually eat at least once or twice or *five* times a day.

So I ask myself, "Why don't I feast on the scriptures more often?" I admit that most of the time I happily anticipate eating food more than I anticipate reading the scriptures and the words of the living prophets. Now you know.

My friend Bonnie Parkin taught about spiritual feasting in a wonderful way: "I want to tell you a secret. I love to eat. Don't you? When food has the perfect herbs, when it's cooked just right, when it's served like a work of sculpture, I'm in heaven. I can gain weight just reading a menu. And did you know that the Lord doesn't expect us to diet? Trust me! Turn to 2 Nephi 9:51. Now look at the very last line. It says, 'Let your soul delight in fatness.' But feast on what? Chocolate? Look closely: Feast on his word. When was the last time you feasted on the word? Did you know that feasting could be so guilt-free?" (*New Era,* November 1996, 33).

Guilt-free feasting: that's a pretty powerful promise! It sounds like a wonderful result of eating something really nutritious, wholesome, and delicious.

The prophet Nephi gave a marvelous promise to all who search the scriptures: "Wherefore, I said unto you, feast upon the words of Christ; for behold, the words of Christ will tell you all things what ye should do" (2 Nephi 32:3).

Why do we sometimes worry so much more about our physical diet than our spiritual diet? We can find a zillion (it *feels* like a zillion) books, magazine and newspaper articles, TV programs, and radio talk shows about carbs and grams of fat and pounds and every conceivable kind of diet. And yet there is one "diet" that, if followed, promises amazing results: the guidance of the Holy Ghost in knowing all things that we should do!

I'm aware of people who read the entire Standard Works every year, and even parts of the Dead Sea Scrolls.

But for most of us, that's beyond our wildest dreams. Just getting in a verse a day is sometimes an accomplishment! I'm comforted by Elder Henry B. Eyring's words: "We may be nourished more by pondering a few words, allowing the Holy Ghost to make them treasures to us, than to pass quickly and superficially over whole chapters of scripture" (*Ensign,* November 1997, 84).

In Sheri Dew's biography of President Gordon B. Hinckley, there's an insight into Sister Marjorie Hinckley that helped me: "Her general outlook, however, was more practical than self-critical. 'I have a new project,' she wrote to Kathy, 'one chapter a day from each of the standard works. I have been on it for four days and am only three days behind. Better to have tried and failed than never to have tried'" (*Go Forward with Faith: The Biography of Gordon B. Hinckley* [Deseret Book, 1996], 346).

I can remember when I was a little girl, not yet twelve, and old people (which was anyone over fifty back then) would make their way to the front of the chapel during testimony meeting and say, with emotion, that they just *loved* the scriptures.

I was sitting back a few rows thinking, "You big fat liar! You don't really mean it. You're just saying that because you think you're supposed to. You're almost *dead,* and you're nervous that if you don't act like you love the scriptures you're not going to get to heaven. . . ."

I would try reading the Book of Mormon. I'd get Lehi and his family out in the wilderness and then get frustrated when they kept going back. That bugged me. Why weren't they *organized?* Wasn't Lehi supposed to be a prophet? Didn't they have a *planner* or something?

I don't know if I got bored or frustrated, but it was a while before I made it through the entire Book of Mormon. I'd just leave Lehi and his family in the wilderness.

I've changed. I've changed my mind. Now I'm one who says that I just love the scriptures, and I really mean it. Has that happened to you in your life?

Interestingly, not one of the places I've ever gone as a missionary had yet had the Book of Mormon translated into the native language. I can't adequately describe the lessons I learned and the deep feelings that came to me as I lived with many who knew the Book of Mormon was the word of God, and bore testimony of that, but had not yet had the privilege of reading it. Imagine! It made me feel embarrassed for my lack of gratitude and attention. When others would ask me, "What does it say?" I'd feel ashamed that I hadn't read more often. I'm being a little hard on myself, but I recognize that I haven't always treated the scriptures with the respect and appreciation they deserve.

I remember an experience in the Philippines in 1964 when my companion and I found a copy of the Bible in Tagalog (one of the major languages of that country) and presented it to dear Brother Ocampo, one of our investigators. As we'd been teaching him, he had mentioned that he'd never had or even held a Bible and thus had not been able to read it himself. We searched stores in Manila until we found one (they're much more readily available now) and took it to him. He got tears in his eyes and accepted it with both hands, then hugged it to him with such joy and tenderness. We also gave him a copy of the Book of Mormon in English, wishing it had already been translated into Tagalog. But that would come later.

By the way, there are now Book of Mormon translations in Mandarin, Cantonese, several languages of the Philippines, Bahasa Indonesia, and Efik, the language of the place I lived in Nigeria, West Africa. And I had the blessing of being in Indonesia when *Kitab Mormon* was completed and members joyfully received their first copies.

In 3 Nephi 10:14 we find a wonderful invitation: "He that hath the scriptures, let him search them." I am one who "hath" the scriptures, and I really enjoy the times when I "search" them.

I'd like to share something President Spencer W. Kimball taught about *why* we feast on the scriptures, and then a few ideas about *how* to do that feasting.

"I find that when I get casual in my relationships with divinity and when it seems that no divine ear is listening and no divine voice is speaking, that I am far, far away. If I immerse myself in the scriptures the distance narrows and the spirituality returns. I find myself loving more intensely those whom I must love with all my heart and mind and strength, and loving them more, I find it easier to abide their counsel" (*The Teachings of Spencer W. Kimball*, 135).

When I'm trying to feast, it helps me so much to meditate and ponder about what I read. I ask myself questions like: "Who's speaking or writing?" "What are the circumstances?" "Why is this being taught?" "How does this help me understand the gospel better?" "What does this mean for MEE?" "What can I learn?" "What can I do better, or differently?" It feels like there's a process wherein words and ideas move from our minds to our hearts. Taking time to ponder helps that process.

Another tip that is helpful is to pray for a testimony of the scriptures, and for understanding. Would it help you to pray before you read? I've found that it *has* made a difference when I've asked Heavenly Father to help me understand what I'm about to read and think about.

Many have shared with me experiences in which they've prayed to find answers in the scriptures to some of their questions and concerns, and sometimes they've opened to a particular page and found verses that were specifically helpful. Perhaps this has happened to you too. When it happens to me, I write the date in my scriptures and then more about the experience in my journal.

I usually read my scriptures in the morning, often reading the words of a hymn or two before I start. (On "brave mornings" I even sing the hymn!) This morning reading gives me good things to think about, and there have been many times when something I've read has been specifically helpful during the day.

I find that it makes a difference for me to read both from the scriptures and from the hymnbook. The First Presidency introduced the 1985 edition of *Hymns* with this counsel: "We hope the hymnbook will take a prominent place among the scriptures and other religious books in our homes. . . . Hymns can lift our spirits, give us courage, and move us to righteous action. They can fill our souls with heavenly thoughts and bring us a spirit of peace. Hymns can also help us withstand the temptations of the adversary. We encourage you to memorize your favorite hymns and study the scriptures that relate to them" (*Hymns of The Church of Jesus Christ of Latter-day Saints* [Salt Lake City: The Church of Jesus Christ of Latter-day Saints, 1985], x).

I also love other Primary songs, and I find them going through my head often. As we sing "I'm Trying to Be Like Jesus," one wonderful way to do that is to seek to apply what we're learning as we search the scriptures. Think of all that happened because Joseph Smith did just this: He read from the book of James in the New Testament, pondered it, and then went to a grove of trees and knelt to pray. As a result, the Restoration happened, with all the beautiful blessings we now have!

As I read and study, I like to "personalize" my scriptures. Sometimes I write comments, ideas, questions, and quotes right in the scriptures. Others have suggested that they keep a journal or notebook where they write their feelings as they read. What wonderful "personal scriptures" these books become!

It can help to look for specific things, like words or themes. An example is to look for the different names and titles for the Savior, or finding all the times the word "remember" is used, particularly in the Book of Mormon, or descriptions of Zion, or whatever else you might be interested in.

Some have shared the idea that it's fun sometimes to go "scripture fishing." Janette Hales Beckham suggests that in a group, such as with your family, you invite everyone to open their scriptures to "wherever" and begin to read. When they come across something that grabs them, everyone stops to listen to what they've found and what meaning it has for them.

And this wonderful counsel comes from Elder M. Russell Ballard: "I encourage you to take time each week to be by yourself, away from television and the crowd. Have your scriptures with you and as you read, ponder, and pray, take an honest look at your life. Evaluate where you stand with the promises you have made with Heavenly Father" (*Ensign,* May 1993, 8).

Sometimes when I quote a scripture I'll start by saying, "This is one of my 1000 favorite verses," and I really mean it. Each time I read the Book of Mormon, for example, I'll get to the beginning of a chapter like 2 Nephi 9 or Mosiah 18 and think, "Oh! This is for sure my favorite!" And I find myself saying that all the way through.

There are times when I like to study two separate passages together, looking for similarities and differences. An example of this is to read and ponder Alma 1:26–31, which describes the establishment of a Zion society. Then compare that to Alma 4:6–12 (not very far away, is it?) where there's a description of how a Zion society is destroyed.

I'm so thankful for the scriptures. I know that if I never feast on them, they'll never be nourishing to me. I know that if I don't make time for personal study and for pondering, I'll miss so much that could be so helpful to me, and so many answers that are just waiting to be found.

So those "old people" weren't lying. They really *did* love the scriptures. And I do too. But I can hear the "young ones" snickering when I get up and say that out loud. I am, after all, well past fifty now.

Dearest Children, God Is Near You

I've been impressed for a long time with the huge mural in the main lobby of the Church Office Building. It's a depiction of the Savior telling His disciples, "Go ye therefore, and teach all nations, baptizing them in the name of the Father, and of the Son, and of the Holy Ghost" (Matthew 28:19).

I look forward to the day when we have a mural portraying the verse that follows: "Teaching them to observe all things whatsoever I have commanded you: and, lo, I am with you alway, even unto the end of the world" (Matthew 28:20).

Let me see if I can explain what I mean. Part of it is taught in the hymn "I Am a Child of God" where we sing, "Teach me all that I must do / To live with him someday" (*Hymns*, no. 301). Blessings are promised to those who live the gospel—who keep the commandments—and sometimes I feel we could do a better job of helping each other figure out how to do this, particularly when it is so new to so many people. The promise in the Book of Mormon (keep my commandments and you will prosper in the land) surely must apply to any of Heavenly Father's children—to those in Africa or Asia or anywhere else.

When I went on my first mission, I had just graduated in nursing from Brigham Young University, and this background allowed me (or compelled me) to notice much in the lives of those I met in Taiwan, Hong Kong, and the Philippines that could be different, better. Many of the things that could make a difference were very simple (washing hands, improving nutrition, giving immunizations). But that was not what I was called to teach.

To receive a call to return to the Philippines in 1972 as a health missionary was a great blessing in my life. It was as if I had been given an opportunity to share more of the fullness of the gospel.

President Joseph F. Smith taught: "It has always been a cardinal teaching with the Latter-day Saints that a religion that has not the power to save people temporally and make them prosperous and happy here cannot be depended upon to save them spiritually and to exalt them in the life to come" (Joseph F. Smith, *Out West,* September 1905, 242).

One of my favorite illustrations of blessings that come from the application of gospel principles is the experience I had with my dear friend Sally. She and her husband had joined the Church in the Philippines with great joy and enthusiasm. As we got acquainted and began teaching topics such as nutrition and child care, Sally told us that they had lost their first child, a little girl, when she was just a few months old. As I remember it, she said the doctor told her the baby wasn't eating right. This was a great sadness for Sally and her husband, because they didn't know some of the things they might have done differently.

Sally had several other children, and now told us that she was once again expecting a baby. She asked us to teach her what she could do in order to have a healthy baby. We all began to call her little one "Mormon Baby." Sally was very receptive to what was shared, and she made some changes in her diet and activity. She would smile and say to me, "Seester, you can never teach an old dog new tricks." Then she'd pause and say, "But Seester, I am not a dog!"

There was great anticipation in the neighborhood as

well as among Church members as the birth of "Mormon Baby" grew close. We as missionaries were praying earnestly that the baby would indeed be born healthy and have a good start in life.

She was born on January 20, 1973, and indeed she was a very healthy, beautiful baby. I remember holding her in Relief Society and asking her to tell us what it was like to anticipate coming to earth, knowing that her parents were doing all they could to prepare for her arrival, including teaching her the gospel. She made such happy sounds that it was like a testimony to us.

I remember a conversation with Sally before Sarah was born. She wondered why some babies and little children seemed so "naughty" in Church meetings compared to the Filipino children. She asked me if I thought it could be that the "naughty" children were better nourished, healthier, and if perhaps the little Filipino children would have loved to be so active and busy. I told her that was a possibility and something we could think about together.

I was so touched when she told me, after Sarah began to grow, "You will be very pleased to know that Mormon Baby is *very* naughty in church!" Of course, what she meant was that her little baby was very healthy!

It has been such a joy through the years to follow the life of Sarah, whose nickname is Little Melon. What a bright little girl! I was able to be there shortly after she was born and through much of her first year. I saw her in 1978 when I was on my way home from a mission in Indonesia, and again in 1981 when I was in the Philippines visiting with welfare missionaries.

When Little Melon was eleven years old, she sent me a letter. Here are a few of her thoughts:

"I'm sorry that I have not written for a long time because every time I'm going to start my letter my playmates are insisting me to play with them. Now I firmly decided to write to you. We are glad that Mommy is doing what the family preparedness program of the welfare missionaries taught them. We now purify our water and have a balance diet, that is why we grow faster than the other children. The Temple is now being made and I hope I'll see you there. I love you. Little Melon"

I received a wonderful letter from her mother, Sally, as well:

"I want to express my gratitude for the things I have learned which are making such a difference in my family. I realize now that some of the things my mother taught me—things her mother taught her—were not correct.

"But the truths I'm learning will now be taught to MY children, and to THEIR children, and to the generations to come. We will not be damned any longer by ignorance.

" 'Ye shall know the truth, and the truth shall make you free!' As they say, it is never too late to learn and change. God must love us dearly to allow us to have so much truth."

Another illustration, simple but beautiful, happened in Africa. My companion, Ann, and I were teaching our incredible neighbor, Cecilia, about safe water. We had asked her to bring some of their drinking water. We had a small magnifying glass, and we talked about the things we can't ordinarily see in our water that could possibly make us sick. As we were looking through the magnifying glass into a glass of their drinking water, we began to see some pretty scary things floating and wiggling.

Her husband, Samuel, arrived and asked what we were doing, so we explained. He asked if he could have a look through the magnifying glass, and we said of course. He was horrified! He asked Cecilia where she had gotten the water, and she explained it was their drinking water.

Samuel ran out the door and began spitting and

coughing. Within a very short time he had begun to put together the first water filter in the whole neighborhood.

As we continued teaching Cecilia lessons she would teach to others, we were talking about safe food and water, and she asked us to stop for a moment. We didn't know why, but of course we stopped. She said, "This is the gospel, isn't it." We wondered what had caused her to make that observation out of the blue, but we didn't want to jump to any conclusions or put words in her mouth. So we just said, "Why do you ask?"

She related that she was feeling the same thing inside her heart and soul as she had when the missionaries had first taught her. This to me was a deep and special confirmation of some of our strongest feelings. The Holy Ghost really does bear witness of *all* that is true. And the gospel is meant to bless us both spiritually and temporally. (By the way, there is something very symbolic about helping people find a way to have safe water. When Jesus talked about "living water," He didn't mean the kind we saw through our magnifying glass!)

In January of 1975 I was in Santiago, Chile, for an unforgettable performance of "Mariquita Cochinita" ("Pigpen Mary"). The branch president had written a two-act musical play based on the little flip-chart story the missionaries used to teach the importance of cleanliness! In the first act, a family was sick and unmotivated, and there were germs (in simple but great costumes) dancing around. In the second act, the family had joined the Church and made many changes in their lives, including cleanliness, and they were happy and healthy. All in attendance clapped and cheered.

During this same month, January of 1975, I was in Bolivia. One unforgettable experience was to be on the Altiplano, which is about 14,000 feet above sea level. (Bolivia's capital city, La Paz, at close to 12,000 feet, is one of the highest cities in the world.)

There I met the Pai family, and oh how I hope I can meet them again someday. We had the blessing of attending their family home evening, and because it was the warmest place in their little home, we were all on the bed. Brother and Sister Pai had been members of the Church for only three months, but when they learned that President Spencer W. Kimball had encouraged members to have gardens, they planted two small vegetable gardens and a flower garden! Each night they covered their three gardens with plastic sheets to protect their treasures from freezing. Can you imagine how Heavenly Father smiled down on them and their little gardens?

Of that experience I wrote in my journal: "The rain and the cold, the walk and the mud were all well worth it. I would have walked one hundred miles to visit with this family and have the privilege of feeling their spirit and their enthusiasm in being members of the Church and learning principles which help them to be healthier and happier."

It *is* a miracle what can happen to Heavenly Father's children as they—WE—do our best to live the gospel. I love the way King Benjamin expressed it: "And moreover, I would desire that ye should consider on the blessed and happy state of those that keep the commandments of God. For behold, they are blessed in all things, both temporal and spiritual; and if they hold out faithful to the end they are received into heaven, that thereby they may dwell with God in a state of never-ending happiness. O remember, remember that these things are true; for the Lord God hath spoken it" (Mosiah 2:41).

My experience has convinced me that the gospel is indeed good news, and that individuals and families are prospered in extraordinary ways as they do their best to keep the commandments. I'm not saying that "prospering" involves money, or even "stuff and things." I'm saying that it means a better life, a happier life, increased peace and contentment, a brightness of hope, knowledge, and intelligence. It's not just *relief,* but a *release* from the dam of ignorance. And ignorance is a terrible dam—ignorance is *not* "bliss." What you don't know *can* hurt you. Thank goodness for the gospel, which encompasses *all* truth, and which really can and does make such a dramatic difference in our lives.

I've seen miracles when I've tried to help people do what they would already have been doing if they had known what, and why, and how. The power is in them. They have been "coping" for a long, long time.

I believe in the little statement: "God helps those who help themselves." But I also believe that "God helps those who cannot help themselves." Isn't it wonderful that we get to help each other? What a beautiful feeling it is to make contributions to fast offering, missionary work, humanitarian efforts, temple building, and the Perpetual Education Fund. What a difference we can help make in individual lives and in the world.

It's like the difference between only giving a man a fish (and sometimes that's what is needed and wanted initially) and teaching him how to fish. And, happily, there is yet another step in the gospel, and that is teaching him how to teach others to fish, and to share fish, and so on.

As stated by Elder Neal A. Maxwell: "The measure of our success is how many have really 'come unto Christ.' The adverse indicators are how many are unbaptized, unordained, unendowed, unsealed, unnourished, uninvolved, and unrighteous. There is plenty for us to do together. In fact, we cannot do the Lord's work effectively unless we do it together" (*Ensign,* September 1987, 75).

The Savior said He came "that they might have life, and that they might have it more abundantly" (John 10:10). I am convinced deep in my soul that He meant this to apply to *all* of Heavenly Father's children. There are millions—no, make that billions—who wait for the good news of the gospel of Jesus Christ, for a reminder of what they agreed to with shouts of joy in a premortal time. Each one is loved dearly and is precious to the Good Shepherd. Jesus has more than enough power and love and experience to understand, succor, comfort, sanctify, rescue, heal, bless, and save.

None of us has a full understanding of what it is we're doing. We're part of something so important—so critical—so sacred in nature. I would like to suggest that we never cease to give our Heavenly Father thanks for what He has allowed us to experience. We have all learned so much from the richness of the temporally poor. We have been enriched and lifted and instructed by them, and by each other.

We still have covenants to keep. We have received opportunities, instruction, and training that few will ever get. There is much expected of us as true "under shepherds." May we all work together toward the day when "God shall wipe away all tears from their eyes; and there shall be no more death, neither sorrow, nor crying, neither shall there be any more pain: for the former things are passed away" (Revelation 21:4).

Enduring to the End

What does it mean to endure? What are some of the things you've endured for a minute? An hour? A year? A lifetime? Maybe some of the hours or even minutes have seemed like a year or a lifetime.

I happen to have been in Paris (actually just at the airport) on Sunday, July 25, 2005, the day Lance Armstrong rode his bike down the Champs-Elysées, winning the Tour de France for the sixth straight time. (And of course he would do it the next year as well, setting a record of seven straight victories.) Incredible!

I cannot imagine how tough this bike race is. I just cannot imagine how tempting it would be to stop, take a drink of cold water, lie down, and just call it quits.

But he *endured!* For three weeks and more than 2000 miles! And really it was more than that, wasn't it? He endured many, many weeks and miles of preparation.

Several years ago, Lance was diagnosed with testicular

cancer, which spread to his lungs and his brain. He was given a 50 percent chance of overcoming the cancer. He not only beat the cancer, but he got himself in shape to race again and has become a superstar; he is considered one of the greatest athletes of all time.

It's great to know of someone like this—a champion, a hero. But the more I've thought about it, the more I've realized that there are all kinds of victories, all kinds of races and challenges, all kinds of opportunities to give all we've got—to *endure.*

Another thing that comes to mind is that during all the hours, days, weeks, months, and years of Lance Armstrong's grueling training, there were no cheering, waving crowds. For the most part, that recognition didn't happen until the actual race. Perhaps some of your bright moments take a long time arriving too. Maybe it seems like "forever."

I know there are many reading this who have endured *much*—and are in the process of enduring as we speak—and could teach me extremely important lessons. We all know of great tragedies, disappointments, and suffering (some of which we know "up close and personal"). I suppose we could all gather together after this life is over and do some "topping" and "bottoming" about who had it hardest, and what it took to endure and survive our particular challenges.

I've thought things like:

- What if a marathon runner quit after 25.5 miles because he (or she) saw a Ben and Jerry's or an inviting patch of shade?
- What if Joseph Smith had gotten discouraged when he was sixteen, or nineteen, or twenty-one, or thirty? What if he'd given up, "gone inactive"?
- What if Elder Neal A. Maxwell had resigned as an Apostle when he found out he had leukemia?
- What if President Hinckley had said he was through when Sister Hinckley went Home?
- What if the Savior had not done what He said He'd do?
- What if missionaries or mothers or fathers or neighbors or any of us were to stop short of victory, of doing what we were meant to do and becoming who we were meant to be?

We're never counseled to "Endure to the middle," or "Endure for quite a while." It's "Endure to the *end*."

I was thinking about this one day, imagining that the

pioneers had become weary and had quit. I imagined a bulletin something like this:

This just in: The Mormon pioneers who were heading West after being driven from the city of Nauvoo have apparently changed their minds. They've halted their trek.

In an exclusive interview, one member of the party said: "This is much more difficult than we had imagined or anticipated. There is no way any of us want to continue. We're tired. We're afraid. We're overwhelmed. There's too much dust some days and mud other days. The rivers are wide, and we'll probably all get West Nile Virus. We've had it. We're not going on. Not even one more mile. We've lost hope. This isn't fun. No one gets excited anymore when it's time to circle the wagons. We've quit dancing, and we've quit singing 'Come, Come, Ye Saints.'"

That's silly, really. Thank goodness they *didn't* give up! Sometimes it helps, doesn't it, to know that others have been brave and strong and true.

There are all kinds of burdens. Sometimes "enduring" lasts for a whole minute, or an hour, or a day or week or longer . . .

For a minute, you may have to endure a headache; waiting for a phone call; standing in line at a store; trying not to be frustrated when you're trapped in traffic.

An hour could find you enduring a final exam, or a physical exam, or being awake in the night, unable to sleep.

A day of enduring could involve waiting for news from or about a loved one, or waiting for the doctor to call with the results of your lab tests.

Several days could be like the experience of Captain Scott O'Grady. Do you remember hearing about him? A U.S. Air Force Captain, he was an F-16 pilot. On June 2, 1995, he was shot down over Bosnia. Amazingly, he survived! For six days he hid, avoiding capture and living on a diet of leaves and insects. Then, in a daring rescue on the morning of June 8, he was picked up by Marine helicopters. He could have given up. It would have been so easy to say, "I can't do this! I'm hungry! I'm thirsty! I give up! Uncle!" Instead, he allowed his life to be changed for the good by his experience. In his words: "I underwent a rebirth. . . . Those six days in Bosnia were a religious retreat for me, a total spiritual renewal. I'm not recommending near-death experience for its own sake; it's a ride I wouldn't care to take again. But I will say that my time in Bosnia was completely positive—nothing bad has come out of it. From the instant that my plane blew up around me, and I opened my heart to God's love, I felt

the most incredible freedom—my joy was unbounded"
(Scott O'Grady with Jeff Coplon, *Return with Honor*
[Doubleday, 1995], 201–2).

A lifetime of enduring could be like the experience of
Helen Keller. I've read her autobiography several times
and am so impressed with her. She became ill as a child
and ended up both blind and deaf. After five years of
darkness and silence, something happened that would
change her life dramatically. Through Dr. Alexander
Graham Bell, she met Miss Anne Sullivan. Anne literally
took young, "wild" Helen Keller by the hand and led her
into life. When she discovered water she later said, "That
living word awakened my soul, gave it light, hope, joy, set
it free! There were barriers still, it is true, but barriers that
could in time be swept away" (Helen Keller, *The Story of
My Life: The Restored Classic* [W.W. Norton, 2003], 28).
Helen learned to speak—in several languages. She graduated with honors from Radcliffe College. She lived a
full, interesting, happy life.

When I think about long-term enduring, I think of
my brother-in-law Wendell Johnson, who lived for thirty-
two years as a quadriplegic. (He was paralyzed from the
neck down as the result of a diving accident when he was
sixteen years old.) He lived an amazingly productive, full

life as a husband, a father, a mayor, an artist, and a wonderful human being.

Our Heavenly Father understands *everything*.

He knows how Wendell felt every single day of those thirty-two years that he spent unable to shoo a fly away or hug his daughter. He knows how *you* are feeling in all the burdens that are so heavy for you right now. He understands your loneliness, your joy, your tears, your heartaches.

God bless you in all that He has asked you to endure. Even though everything and everyone else might fail, *He never will*. "They that wait upon the Lord shall renew their strength; they shall mount up with wings as eagles; they shall run, and not be weary; and they shall walk, and not faint" (Isaiah 40:31).

I know that as we call out to Him for help, He will find someone to come and help us. May we endure together until we are all safely back Home.